# MAKING SENSE OF THE
# BIBLE

## Works by Wayne Grudem

*Bible Doctrine: Essential Teachings of the Christian Faith*

*Christian Beliefs: Twenty Basics Every Christian Should Know*

*Counterpoints: Are Miraculous Gifts for Today? (General Editor)*

*Politics According to the Bible*

*Systematic Theology*

*Systematic Theology Laminated Sheet*

### Making Sense of Series

*Making Sense of the Bible*

*Making Sense of Who God Is*

*Making Sense of Man and Sin*

*Making Sense of Christ and the Spirit*

*Making Sense of Salvation*

*Making Sense of the Church*

*Making Sense of the Future*

# MAKING SENSE OF THE
# BIBLE

## ONE OF SEVEN PARTS FROM GRUDEM'S
### *SYSTEMATIC THEOLOGY*

# WAYNE GRUDEM

ZONDERVAN®

ZONDERVAN.com/
AUTHORTRACKER
*follow your favorite authors*

ZONDERVAN

*Making Sense of the Bible*
Copyright © 1994, 2011 by Wayne Grudem

Previously published in *Systematic Theology*

This title is also available as a Zondervan ebook. Visit www.zondervan.com/ebooks.

Requests for information should be addressed to:

Zondervan, *Grand Rapids, Michigan* 49530

This edition: ISBN  978-0-310-49311-2 (softcover)

The Library of Congress has cataloged the complete volume as:

Grudem, Wayne Arden.
    Systematic theology: an introduction to biblical doctrine / Wayne Grudem.
       p.   cm.
    Includes index.
    ISBN  978-0-310-28670-7
    1. Theology, Doctrinal. I. Title.
  BT75.2.G78 — 1994
  230'.046—dc20                                  94-8300

Cover design: *Rob Monacelli*
Interior design: *Mark Sheeres*

*Printed in the United States of America*

14 15 16 /DCI/ 33 32 31 30 29 28 27 26 25 24 23 22 21 20 19 18 17 16 15 14 13 12 11 10 9 8 7 6 5 4 3

# CONTENTS

# PREFACE

I have not written this book for other teachers of theology (though I hope many of them will read it). I have written it for students—and not only for students, but also for every Christian who has a hunger to know the central doctrines of the Bible in greater depth.

I have tried to make it understandable even for Christians who have never studied theology before. I have avoided using technical terms without first explaining them. And most of the chapters can be read on their own, so that someone can begin at any chapter and grasp it without having read the earlier material.

Introductory studies do not have to be shallow or simplistic. I am convinced that most Christians are able to understand the doctrinal teachings of the Bible in considerable depth, provided that they are presented clearly and without the use of highly technical language. Therefore I have not hesitated to treat theological disputes in some detail where it seemed necessary.

Yet this book is still an *introduction* to systematic theology. Entire books have been written about the topics covered in each chapter of this book, and entire articles have been written about many of the verses quoted in this book. Therefore each chapter is capable of opening out into additional study in more breadth or more depth for those who are interested. The bibliographies at the end of each chapter give some help in that direction.

The following six distinctive features of this book grow out of my convictions about what systematic theology is and how it should be taught:

**1. A Clear Biblical Basis for Doctrines.** Because I believe that theology should be explicitly based on the teachings of Scripture, in each chapter I have attempted to show where the Bible gives support for the doctrines under consideration. In fact, because I believe that the words of Scripture themselves have power and authority greater than any human words, I have not just given Bible references; I have frequently quoted Bible passages at length so that readers can easily examine for themselves the scriptural evidence and in that way be like the noble Bereans, who were "examining the scriptures daily to see if these things were so" (Acts 17:11). This conviction about the unique nature of the Bible as God's words has also led to the inclusion of a Scripture memory passage at the end of each chapter.

**2. Clarity in the Explanation of Doctrines.** I do not believe that God intended the study of theology to result in confusion and frustration. A student who comes out of a course in theology filled only with doctrinal uncertainty and a thousand unanswered questions is hardly "able to give instruction in sound doctrine and also to confute those who contradict it" (Titus 1:9). Therefore I have tried to state the doctrinal positions of this book clearly and to show where in Scripture I find convincing evidence for those positions. I do not expect that everyone reading this book will agree with me at every point of doctrine; I do think that every reader will understand the positions I am arguing for and where Scripture can be found to support those positions.

This does not mean that I ignore other views. Where there are doctrinal differences within evangelical Christianity I have tried to represent other positions fairly, to explain why I disagree with them, and to give references to the best available defenses of the opposing positions. In fact, I have made it easy for students to find a conservative evangelical statement on each topic from within their own theological traditions, because each chapter contains an index to treatments of that chapter's subject in thirty-four other theology texts classified by denominational background.

**3. Application to Life.** I do not believe that God intended the study of theology to be dry and boring. Theology is the study of God and all his works! Theology is meant to be lived and prayed and sung! All of the great doctrinal writings of the Bible (such as Paul's epistle to the Romans) are full of praise to God and personal application to life. For this reason I have incorporated notes on application from time to time in the text, and have added "Questions for Personal Application" at the end of each chapter, as well as a hymn related to the topic of the chapter. True theology is "teaching which accords with godliness" (1 Tim. 6:3), and theology when studied rightly will lead to growth in our Christian lives, and to worship.

**4. Focus on the Evangelical World.** I do not think that a true system of theology can be constructed from within what we may call the "liberal" theological tradition—that is, by people who deny the absolute truthfulness of the Bible, or who do not think the words of the Bible to be God's very words. For this reason, the other writers I interact with in this book are mostly within what is today called the larger "conservative evangelical" tradition—from the great Reformers John Calvin and Martin Luther, down to the writings of evangelical scholars today. I write as an evangelical and for evangelicals. This does not mean that those in the liberal tradition have nothing valuable to say; it simply means that differences with them almost always boil down to differences over the nature of the Bible and its authority. The amount of doctrinal agreement that can be reached by people with widely divergent bases of authority is quite limited. I am thankful for my evangelical friends who write extensive critiques of liberal theology, but I do not think that everyone is called to do that, or that an extensive analysis of liberal views is the most helpful way to build a positive system of theology based on the total truthfulness of the whole Bible. In fact, somewhat like the boy in Hans Christian Andersen's tale who shouted, "The Emperor has no clothes!" I think someone needs to say that it is doubtful that liberal theologians have given us any significant insights into the doctrinal teachings of Scripture that are not already to be found in evangelical writers.

It is not always appreciated that the world of conservative evangelical scholarship is so rich and diverse that it affords ample opportunity for exploration of different viewpoints and insights into Scripture. I think that ultimately we will attain much more depth of understanding of Scripture when we are able to study it in the company of a great number of scholars who all begin with the conviction that the Bible is completely true and absolutely authoritative. The cross-references to thirty-four other evangelical systematic theologies that I have put at the end of each chapter reflect this conviction: though they are broken down into seven broad theological traditions (Anglican/Episcopalian, Arminian/Wesleyan/Methodist, Baptist, Dispensational, Lutheran, Reformed/Presbyterian, and Renewal/Charismatic/ Pentecostal), they all would hold to the inerrancy of the Bible and would belong to what would be called a conservative evangelical position today. (In addition to these thirty-four conservative evangelical works, I have also added to each chapter a section of cross-references to two representative Roman Catholic theologies, because Roman Catholicism continues to exercise such a significant influence worldwide.)

**5. Hope for Progress in Doctrinal Unity in the Church.** I believe that there is still much hope for the church to attain deeper and purer doctrinal understanding, and to overcome old barriers, even those that have persisted for centuries. Jesus is at work perfecting his church "that he might present the church to himself in splendor, without spot or wrinkle or any such thing, that she might be holy and without blemish" (Eph. 5:27), and he has given gifts to equip the church "until we all attain to the unity of the faith and of the knowledge of the Son of God" (Eph. 4:13). Though the past history of the church may discourage us, these Scriptures remain true, and we should not abandon hope of greater agreement. In fact, in this century we have already seen much greater understanding and some greater doctrinal agreement between Covenant and Dispensational theologians, and between charismatics and noncharismatics; moreover, I think the church's understanding of biblical inerrancy and of spiritual gifts has also increased significantly in the last few decades. I believe that the current debate over appropriate roles for men and women in marriage and the church will eventually result in much greater understanding of the teaching of Scripture as well, painful though the controversy may be at the present time. Therefore, in this book I have not hesitated to raise again some of the old differences (over baptism, the Lord's Supper, church government, the millennium and the tribulation, and predestination, for example) in the hope that, in some cases at least, a fresh look at Scripture may provoke a new examination of these doctrines and may perhaps prompt some movement not just toward greater understanding and tolerance of other viewpoints, but even toward greater doctrinal consensus in the church.

**6. A Sense of the Urgent Need for Greater Doctrinal Understanding in the Whole Church.** I am convinced that there is an urgent need in the church today for much greater understanding of Christian doctrine, or systematic theology. Not only pastors and teachers need to understand theology in greater depth—the whole church does as well. One day by God's grace we may have churches full of Christians who can discuss, apply, and live the doctrinal teachings of the Bible as readily as they can discuss the details of their own jobs or hobbies—or the fortunes of their favorite sports team or television program. It is not that Christians lack the ability to understand doctrine; it is just that they must have access to it in an understandable form. Once that happens, I think that many Christians will find that understanding (and living) the doctrines of Scripture is one of their greatest joys.

> *"O give thanks to the LORD, for he is good; for his steadfast love endures for ever!" (Ps. 118:29).*

> *"Not to us, O LORD, not to us, but to your name give glory" (Ps. 115:1).*

WAYNE GRUDEM
Phoenix Seminary
4222 E. Thomas Road/Suite 400
Phoenix, Arizona 85018
USA

# ABBREVIATIONS

| | |
|---|---|
| BAGD | *A Greek-English Lexicon of the New Testament and Other Early Christian Literature.* Ed. Walter Bauer. Rev. and trans. Wm. Arndt, F. W. Gingrich, and F. Danker. Chicago: University of Chicago Press, 1979. |
| BDB | *A Hebrew and English Lexicon of the Old Testament.* F. Brown, S. R. Driver, and C. Briggs. Oxford: Clarendon Press, 1907; reprinted, with corrections, 1968. |
| BETS | *Bulletin of the Evangelical Theological Society* |
| BibSac | *Bibliotheca Sacra* |
| cf. | compare |
| CRSQ | *Creation Research Society Quarterly* |
| CT | *Christianity Today* |
| CThRev | *Criswell Theological Review* |
| DPCM | *Dictionary of Pentecostal and Charismatic Movements.* Stanley M. Burgess and Gary B. McGee, eds. Grand Rapids: Zondervan, 1988. |
| EBC | *Expositor's Bible Commentary.* Frank E. Gaebelein, ed. Grand Rapids: Zondervan, 1976. |
| ed. | edited by, edition |
| EDT | *Evangelical Dictionary of Theology.* Walter Elwell, ed. Grand Rapids: Baker, 1984. |
| et al. | and others |
| IBD | *The Illustrated Bible Dictionary.* Ed. J. D. Douglas, et al. 3 vols. Leicester: Inter-Varsity Press, and Wheaton: Tyndale House, 1980. |
| ISBE | *International Standard Bible Encyclopedia.* Revised edition. G. W. Bromiley, ed. Grand Rapids: Eerdmans, 1982. |
| JAMA | *Journal of the American Medical Association* |
| JBL | *Journal of Biblical Literature* |
| JETS | *Journal of the Evangelical Theological Society* |
| JSOT | *Journal for the Study of the Old Testament* |
| KJV | King James Version (Authorized Version) |
| LSJ | *A Greek-English Lexicon,* ninth edition. Henry Liddell, Robert Scott, H. S. Jones, R. McKenzie. Oxford: Clarendon Press, 1940. |
| LXX | Septuagint |
| mg. | margin or marginal notes |
| n. | note |
| n.d. | no date of publication given |
| n.p. | no place of publication given |

| NASB | New American Standard Bible |
| NDT | *New Dictionary of Theology.* S. B. Ferguson, D. F. Wright, J. I. Packer, eds. Leicester and Downers Grove, Ill.: InterVarsity Press, 1988. |
| NIDCC | *New International Dictionary of the Christian Church.* Ed. J. D. Douglas et al. Grand Rapids: Zondervan, 1974. |
| NIDNTT | *The New International Dictionary of New Testament Theology.* 3 vols. Colin Brown, gen. ed. Grand Rapids: Zondervan, 1975–78. |
| NIGTC | New International Greek Testament Commentaries |
| NIV | New International Version |
| NKJV | New King James Version |
| NTS | *New Testament Studies* |
| ODCC | *Oxford Dictionary of the Christian Church.* Ed. F. L. Cross. London and New York: Oxford University Press, 1977. |
| rev. | revised |
| RSV | Revised Standard Version |
| TB | *Tyndale Bulletin* |
| TDNT | *Theological Dictionary of the New Testament.* 10 vols. G. Kittel and G. Friedrich, eds.; trans. G. W. Bromiley. Grand Rapids: Eerdmans, 1964–76. |
| TNTC | Tyndale New Testament Commentaries |
| TOTC | Tyndale Old Testament Commentaries |
| trans. | translated by |
| TrinJ | *Trinity Journal* |
| vol. | volume |
| WBC | Word Biblical Commentary |
| WTJ | *Westminster Theological Journal* |

# Chapter 1

# INTRODUCTION TO SYSTEMATIC THEOLOGY

*What is systematic theology?*
*Why should Christians study it?*
*How should we study it?*

## EXPLANATION AND SCRIPTURAL BASIS

### A. Definition of Systematic Theology

What is systematic theology? Many different definitions have been given, but for the purposes of this book the following definition will be used: *Systematic theology is any study that answers the question, "What does the whole Bible teach us today?" about any given topic.*[1]

This definition indicates that systematic theology involves collecting and understanding all the relevant passages in the Bible on various topics and then summarizing their teachings clearly so that we know what to believe about each topic.

**1. Relationship to Other Disciplines.** The emphasis of this book will not therefore be on *historical theology* (a historical study of how Christians in different periods have understood various theological topics) or *philosophical theology* (studying theological topics largely without use of the Bible, but using the tools and methods of philosophical reasoning and what can be known about God from observing the universe) or *apologetics*

---

[1]This definition of systematic theology is taken from Professor John Frame, now of Westminster Seminary in Escondido, California, under whom I was privileged to study in 1971–73 (at Westminster Seminary, Philadelphia). Though it is impossible to acknowledge my indebtedness to him at every point, it is appropriate to express gratitude to him at this point, and to say that he has probably influenced my theological thinking more than anyone else, especially in the crucial areas of the nature of systematic theology and the doctrine of the Word of God. Many of his former students will recognize echoes of his teaching in the following pages, especially in those two areas.

(providing a defense of the truthfulness of the Christian faith for the purpose of convincing unbelievers). These three subjects, which are worthwhile subjects for Christians to pursue, are sometimes also included in a broader definition of the term *systematic theology*. In fact, some consideration of historical, philosophical, and apologetic matters will be found at points throughout this book. This is because historical study informs us of the insights gained and the mistakes made by others previously in understanding Scripture; philosophical study helps us understand right and wrong thought forms common in our culture and others; and apologetic study helps us bring the teachings of Scripture to bear on the objections raised by unbelievers. But these areas of study are not the focus of this volume, which rather interacts directly with the biblical text in order to understand what the Bible itself says to us about various theological subjects.

If someone prefers to use the term *systematic theology* in the broader sense just mentioned instead of the narrow sense which has been defined above, it will not make much difference.[2] Those who use the narrower definition will agree that these other areas of study definitely contribute in a positive way to our understanding of systematic theology, and those who use the broader definition will certainly agree that historical theology, philosophical theology, and apologetics can be distinguished from the process of collecting and synthesizing all the relevant Scripture passages for various topics. Moreover, even though historical and philosophical studies do contribute to our understanding of theological questions, only Scripture has the final authority to define what we are to believe,[3] and it is therefore appropriate to spend some time focusing on the process of analyzing the teaching of Scripture itself.

Systematic theology, as we have defined it, also differs from *Old Testament theology*, *New Testament theology*, and *biblical theology*. These three disciplines organize their topics historically and in the order the topics are presented in the Bible. Therefore, in Old Testament theology, one might ask, "What does Deuteronomy teach about prayer?" or "What do the Psalms teach about prayer?" or "What does Isaiah teach about prayer?" or even, "What does the whole Old Testament teach about prayer and how is that teaching developed over the history of the Old Testament?" In New Testament theology one might ask, "What does John's gospel teach about prayer?" or "What does Paul teach about prayer?" or even "What does the New Testament teach about prayer and what is the historical development of that teaching as it progresses through the New Testament?"

"Biblical theology" has a technical meaning in theological studies. It is the larger category that contains both Old Testament theology and New Testament theology as we have defined them above. Biblical theology gives special attention to the teachings of *individual authors and sections* of Scripture, and to the place of each teaching in the *historical development* of Scripture.[4] So one might ask, "What is the historical development

---

[2]Gordon Lewis and Bruce Demarest have coined a new phrase, "integrative theology," to refer to systematic theology in this broader sense: see their excellent work, *Integrative Theology* (Grand Rapids: Zondervan, 1996). For each doctrine, they analyze historical alternatives and relevant biblical passages, give a coherent summary of the doctrine, answer philosophical objections, and give practical application.

[3]Charles Hodge says, "The Scriptures contain all the Facts of Theology" (section heading in *Systematic Theology*, 1:15). He argues that ideas gained from intuition or observation or experience are valid in theology only if they are supported by the teaching of Scripture.

[4]The term "biblical theology" might seem to be a natural and appropriate one for the process I have called

of the teaching about prayer as it is seen throughout the history of the Old Testament and then of the New Testament?" Of course, this question comes very close to the question, "What does the whole Bible teach us today about prayer?" (which would be *systematic theology* by our definition). It then becomes evident that the boundary lines between these various disciplines often overlap at the edges, and parts of one study blend into the next. Yet there is still a difference, for biblical theology traces the historical development of a doctrine and the way in which one's place at some point in that historical development affects one's understanding and application of that particular doctrine. Biblical theology also focuses on the understanding of each doctrine that the biblical authors and their original hearers or readers possessed.

Systematic theology, on the other hand, makes use of the material of biblical theology and often builds on the results of biblical theology. At some points, especially where great detail and care is needed in the development of a doctrine, systematic theology will even use a biblical-theological method, analyzing the development of each doctrine through the historical development of Scripture. But the focus of systematic theology remains different: its focus is on the collection and then the summary of the teaching of all the biblical passages on a particular subject. Thus systematic theology asks, for example, "What does the whole Bible teach us today about prayer?" It attempts to summarize the teaching of Scripture in a brief, understandable, and very carefully formulated statement.

**2. Application to Life.** Furthermore, systematic theology focuses on summarizing each doctrine as it should be understood by present-day Christians. This will sometimes involve the use of terms and even concepts that were not themselves used by any individual biblical author, but that are the proper result of combining the teachings of two or more biblical authors on a particular subject. The terms *Trinity, incarnation,* and *deity of Christ,* for example, are not found in the Bible, but they usefully summarize biblical concepts.

Defining systematic theology to include "what the whole Bible *teaches us* today" implies that application to life is a necessary part of the proper pursuit of systematic theology. Thus a doctrine under consideration is seen in terms of its practical value for living the Christian life. Nowhere in Scripture do we find doctrine studied for its own sake or in isolation from life. The biblical writers consistently apply their teaching to life. Therefore, any Christian reading this book should find his or her Christian life enriched and deepened during this study; indeed, if personal spiritual growth does not occur, then the book has not been written properly by the author or the material has not been rightly studied by the reader.

**3. Systematic Theology and Disorganized Theology.** If we use this definition of systematic theology, it will be seen that most Christians actually do systematic theology (or at least make systematic-theological statements) many times a week. For example: "The Bible says that everyone who believes in Jesus Christ will be saved." "The Bible says

---

"systematic theology." However, its usage in theological studies to refer to tracing the historical development of doctrines throughout the Bible is too well established, so that starting now to use the term biblical theology to refer to what I have called systematic theology would only result in confusion.

that Jesus Christ is the only way to God." "The Bible says that Jesus is coming again." These are all summaries of what Scripture says and, as such, they are systematic-theological statements. In fact, every time a Christian says something about what the whole Bible says, he or she is in a sense doing "systematic theology"—according to our definition—by thinking about various topics and answering the question, "What does the whole Bible teach us today?"[5]

How then does this book differ from the "systematic theology" that most Christians do? First, it treats biblical topics in a *carefully organized way* to guarantee that all important topics will receive thorough consideration. This organization also provides one sort of check against inaccurate analysis of individual topics, for it means that all other doctrines that are treated can be compared with each topic for consistency in methodology and absence of contradictions in the relationships between the doctrines. This also helps to ensure balanced consideration of complementary doctrines: Christ's deity and humanity are studied together, for example, as are God's sovereignty and man's responsibility, so that wrong conclusions will not be drawn from an imbalanced emphasis on only one aspect of the full biblical presentation.

In fact, the adjective *systematic* in systematic theology should be understood to mean something like "carefully organized by topics," with the understanding that the topics studied will be seen to fit together in a consistent way, and will include all the major doctrinal topics of the Bible. Thus "systematic" should be thought of as the opposite of "randomly arranged" or "disorganized." In systematic theology topics are treated in an orderly or "systematic" way.

A second difference between this book and the way most Christians do systematic theology is that it treats topics in *much more detail* than most Christians do. For example, an ordinary Christian as a result of regular reading of the Bible may make the theological statement, "The Bible says that everyone who believes in Jesus Christ will be saved." That is a perfectly true summary of a major biblical teaching. However, it can take several pages to elaborate more precisely what it means to "believe in Jesus Christ," and it could take several chapters to explain what it means to "be saved" in all of the many implications of that term.

Third, a formal study of systematic theology will make it possible to formulate summaries of biblical teachings with *much more accuracy* than Christians would normally arrive at without such a study. In systematic theology, summaries of biblical teachings must be worded precisely to guard against misunderstandings and to exclude false teachings.

Fourth, a good theological analysis must find and treat fairly *all the relevant Bible passages* for each particular topic, not just some or a few of the relevant passages. This

---

[5]Robert L. Reymond, "The Justification of Theology with a Special Application to Contemporary Christology," in Nigel M. Cameron, ed., *The Challenge of Evangelical Theology: Essays in Approach and Method* (Edinburgh: Rutherford House, 1987), pp. 82–104, cites several examples from the New Testament of this kind of searching through all of Scripture to demonstrate doctrinal conclusions: Jesus in Luke 24:25–27 (and elsewhere); Apollos in Acts 18:28; the Jerusalem Council in Acts 15; and Paul in Acts 17:2–3; 20:27; and all of Romans. To this list could be added Heb. 1 (on Christ's divine Sonship), Heb. 11 (on the nature of true faith), and many other passages from the Epistles.

often means that it must depend on the results of careful exegesis (or interpretation) of Scripture generally agreed upon by evangelical interpreters or, where there are significant differences of interpretation, systematic theology will include detailed exegesis at certain points.

Because of the large number of topics covered in a study of systematic theology and because of the great detail with which these topics are analyzed, it is inevitable that someone studying a systematic theology text or taking a course in systematic theology for the first time will have many of his or her own personal beliefs challenged or modified, refined or enriched. It is of utmost importance therefore that each person beginning such a course firmly resolve in his or her own mind to abandon as false any idea which is found to be clearly contradicted by the teaching of Scripture. But it is also very important for each person to resolve not to believe any individual doctrine simply because this textbook or some other textbook or teacher says that it is true, unless this book or the instructor in a course can convince the student from the text of Scripture itself. It is Scripture alone, not "conservative evangelical tradition" or any other human authority, that must function as the normative authority for the definition of what we should believe.

**4. What Are Doctrines?** In this book, the word *doctrine* will be understood in the following way: *A doctrine is what the whole Bible teaches us today about some particular topic.* This definition is directly related to our earlier definition of systematic theology, since it shows that a "doctrine" is simply the result of the process of doing systematic theology with regard to one particular topic. Understood in this way, doctrines can be very broad or very narrow. We can speak of "the doctrine of God" as a major doctrinal category, including a summary of all that the Bible teaches us today about God. Such a doctrine would be exceptionally large. On the other hand, we may also speak more narrowly of the doctrine of God's eternity, or the doctrine of the Trinity, or the doctrine of God's justice.[6]

Within the major doctrinal category of this book, many more specific teachings have been selected as appropriate for inclusion. Generally these meet at least one of the following three criteria: (1) they are doctrines that are most emphasized in Scripture; (2) they are doctrines that have been most significant throughout the history of the church and have been important for all Christians at all times; (3) they are doctrines that have become important for Christians in the present situation in the history of the church (even though some of these doctrines may not have been of such great interest earlier in church history). Some examples of doctrines in the third category would be the doctrine of the inerrancy of Scripture, the doctrine of baptism in the Holy Spirit, the doctrine of Satan and demons with particular reference to spiritual warfare, the doctrine of spiritual gifts in the New Testament age, and the doctrine of the creation of man as male and female in relation to the understanding of roles appropriate to men and women today.

---

[6]The word *dogma* is an approximate synonym for *doctrine,* but I have not used it in this book. *Dogma* is a term more often used by Roman Catholic and Lutheran theologians, and the term frequently refers to doctrines that have official church endorsement. *Dogmatic theology* is another term for *systematic theology.*

Finally, what is the difference between systematic theology and *Christian ethics?* Although there is inevitably some overlap between the study of theology and the study of ethics, I have tried to maintain a distinction in emphasis. The emphasis of systematic theology is on what God wants us to *believe* and to *know,* while the emphasis in Christian ethics is on what God wants us to *do* and what *attitudes* he wants us to have. Such a distinction is reflected in the following definition: *Christian ethics is any study that answers the question, "What does God require us to do and what attitudes does he require us to have today?" with regard to any given situation.* Thus theology focuses on ideas while ethics focuses on situations in life. Theology tells us how we should think while ethics tells us how we should live. A textbook on ethics, for example, would discuss topics such as marriage and divorce, lying and telling the truth, stealing and ownership of property, abortion, birth control, homosexuality, the role of civil government, discipline of children, capital punishment, war, care for the poor, racial discrimination, and so forth. Of course there is some overlap: theology must be applied to life (therefore it is often ethical to some degree). And ethics must be based on proper ideas of God and his world (therefore it is theological to some degree).

This book will emphasize systematic theology, though it will not hesitate to apply theology to life where such application comes readily. Still, for a thorough treatment of Christian ethics, another textbook similar to this in scope would be necessary.

## B. Initial Assumptions of This Book

We begin with two assumptions or presuppositions: (1) that the Bible is true and that it is, in fact, our only absolute standard of truth; (2) that the God who is spoken of in the Bible exists, and that he is who the Bible says he is: the Creator of heaven and earth and all things in them. These two presuppositions, of course, are always open to later adjustment or modification or deeper confirmation, but at this point, these two assumptions form the point at which we begin.

## C. Why Should Christians Study Theology?

Why should Christians study systematic theology? That is, why should we engage in the process of collecting and summarizing the teachings of many individual Bible passages on particular topics? Why is it not sufficient simply to continue reading the Bible regularly every day of our lives?

**1. The Basic Reason.** Many answers have been given to this question, but too often they leave the impression that systematic theology somehow can "improve" on the Bible by doing a better job of organizing its teachings or explaining them more clearly than the Bible itself has done. Thus we may begin implicitly to deny the clarity of Scripture or the sufficiency of Scripture.

However, Jesus commanded his disciples and now commands us also to *teach* believers to observe all that he commanded:

> Go therefore and make disciples of all nations, baptizing them in the name of the Father and of the Son and of the Holy Spirit, *teaching them* to observe all

that I have commanded you; and lo, I am with you always, to the close of the age. (Matt. 28:19–20)

Now to teach all that Jesus commanded, in a narrow sense, is simply to teach the content of the oral teaching of Jesus as it is recorded in the gospel narratives. However, in a broader sense, "all that Jesus commanded" includes the interpretation and application of his life and teachings, because in the book of Acts it is implied that it contains a narrative of what Jesus *continued* to do and teach through the apostles after his resurrection (note that 1:1 speaks of "all that Jesus *began* to do and teach"). "All that Jesus commanded" can also include the Epistles, since they were written under the supervision of the Holy Spirit and were also considered to be a "command of the Lord" (1 Cor. 14:37; see also John 14:26; 16:13; 1 Thess. 4:15; 2 Peter 3:2; and Rev. 1:1–3). Thus in a larger sense, "all that Jesus commanded" includes all of the New Testament.

Furthermore, when we consider that the New Testament writings endorse the absolute confidence Jesus had in the authority and reliability of the Old Testament Scriptures as God's words, and when we realize that the New Testament epistles also endorse this view of the Old Testament as absolutely authoritative words of God, then it becomes evident that we cannot teach "all that Jesus commanded" without including all of the Old Testament (rightly understood in the various ways in which it applies to the new covenant age in the history of redemption) as well.

The task of fulfilling the Great Commission includes therefore not only evangelism but also *teaching*. And the task of teaching all that Jesus commanded us is, in a broad sense, the task of teaching what the whole Bible says to us today. To effectively teach ourselves and to teach others what the whole Bible says, it is necessary to *collect* and *summarize* all the Scripture passages on a particular subject.

For example, if someone asks me, "What does the Bible teach about Christ's return?" I could say, "Just keep reading your Bible and you'll find out." But if the questioner begins reading at Genesis 1:1 it will be a long time before he or she finds the answer to his question. By that time many other questions will have needed answers, and his list of unanswered questions will begin to grow very long indeed. What does the Bible teach about the work of the Holy Spirit? What does the Bible teach about prayer? What does the Bible teach about sin? There simply is not time in our lifetimes to read through the entire Bible looking for an answer for ourselves every time a doctrinal question arises. Therefore, for us to learn what the Bible says, it is very helpful to have the benefit of the work of others who have searched through Scripture and found answers to these various topics.

We can teach others most effectively if we can direct them to the most relevant passages and suggest an appropriate summary of the teachings of those passages. Then the person who questions us can inspect those passages quickly for himself or herself and learn much more rapidly what the teaching of the Bible is on a particular subject. Thus the necessity of systematic theology for teaching what the Bible says comes about primarily because we are finite in our memory and in the amount of time at our disposal.

The basic reason for studying systematic theology, then, is that it enables us to teach ourselves and others what the whole Bible says, thus fulfilling the second part of the Great Commission.

**2. The Benefits to Our Lives.** Although the basic reason for studying systematic theology is that it is a means of obedience to our Lord's command, there are some additional specific benefits that come from such study.

First, studying theology helps us *overcome our wrong ideas.* If there were no sin in our hearts, we could read the Bible from cover to cover and, although we would not immediately learn everything in the Bible, we would most likely learn only true things about God and his creation. Every time we read it we would learn more true things and we would not rebel or refuse to accept anything we found written there. But with sin in our hearts we retain some rebelliousness against God. At various points there are — for all of us — biblical teachings which for one reason or another we do not want to accept. The study of systematic theology is of help in overcoming those rebellious ideas.

For example, suppose there is someone who does not want to believe that Jesus is personally coming back to earth again. We could show this person one verse or perhaps two that speak of Jesus' return to earth, but the person might still find a way to evade the force of those verses or read a different meaning into them. But if we collect twenty-five or thirty verses that say that Jesus is coming back to earth personally and write them all out on paper, our friend who hesitated to believe in Christ's return is much more likely to be persuaded by the breadth and diversity of biblical evidence for this doctrine. Of course, we all have areas like that, areas where our understanding of the Bible's teaching is inadequate. In these areas, it is helpful for us to be confronted with the *total weight of the teaching of Scripture* on that subject, so that we will more readily be persuaded even against our initial wrongful inclinations.

Second, studying systematic theology helps us to be *able to make better decisions later* on new questions of doctrine that may arise. We cannot know what new doctrinal controversies will arise in the churches in which we will live and minister ten, twenty, or thirty years from now, if the Lord does not return before then. These new doctrinal controversies will sometimes include questions that no one has faced very carefully before. Christians will be asking, "What does the whole Bible say about this subject?" (The precise nature of biblical inerrancy and the appropriate understanding of biblical teaching on gifts of the Holy Spirit are two examples of questions that have arisen in our century with much more forcefulness than ever before in the history of the church.)

Whatever the new doctrinal controversies are in future years, those who have learned systematic theology well will be much better able to answer the new questions that arise. The reason for this is that everything that the Bible says is somehow related to everything else the Bible says (for it all fits together in a consistent way, at least within God's own understanding of reality, and in the nature of God and creation as they really are). Thus the new question will be related to much that has already been learned from Scripture. The more thoroughly that earlier material has been learned, the better able we will be to deal with those new questions.

This benefit extends even more broadly. We face problems of applying Scripture to life in many more contexts than formal doctrinal discussions. What does the Bible teach about husband-wife relationships? About raising children? About witnessing to a friend at work? What principles does Scripture give us for studying psychology, or economics, or the natural sciences? How does it guide us in spending money, or in saving, or in tithing? In every area of inquiry certain theological principles will come to bear, and those who have learned well the theological teachings of the Bible will be much better able to make decisions that are pleasing to God.

A helpful analogy at this point is that of a jigsaw puzzle. If the puzzle represents "what the whole Bible teaches us today about everything" then a course in systematic theology would be like filling in the border and some of the major items pictured in the puzzle. But we will never know everything that the Bible teaches about everything, so our jigsaw puzzle will have many gaps, many pieces that remain to be put in. Solving a new real-life problem is analogous to filling in another section of the jigsaw puzzle: the more pieces one has in place correctly to begin with, the easier it is to fit new pieces in, and the less apt one is to make mistakes. In this book the goal is to enable Christians to put into their "theological jigsaw puzzle" as many pieces with as much accuracy as possible, and to encourage Christians to go on putting in more and more correct pieces for the rest of their lives. The Christian doctrines studied here will act as guidelines to help in the filling in of all other areas, areas that pertain to all aspects of truth in all aspects of life.

Third, studying systematic theology will *help us grow as Christians.* The more we know about God, about his Word, about his relationships to the world and mankind, the better we will trust him, the more fully we will praise him, and the more readily we will obey him. Studying systematic theology rightly will make us more mature Christians. If it does not do this, we are not studying it in the way God intends.

In fact, the Bible often connects sound doctrine with maturity in Christian living: Paul speaks of "*the teaching which accords with godliness*" (1 Tim. 6:3) and says that his work as an apostle is "to further the faith of God's elect and their knowledge of *the truth which accords with godliness*" (Titus 1:1). By contrast, he indicates that all kinds of disobedience and immorality are "contrary to sound doctrine" (1 Tim. 1:10).

In connection with this idea it is appropriate to ask what the difference is between a "major doctrine" and a "minor doctrine." Christians often say they want to seek agreement in the church on major doctrines but also to allow for differences on minor doctrines. I have found the following guideline useful:

> A major doctrine is one that has a significant impact on our thinking about other doctrines, or that has a significant impact on how we live the Christian life. A minor doctrine is one that has very little impact on how we think about other doctrines, and very little impact on how we live the Christian life.

By this standard doctrines such as the authority of the Bible, the Trinity, the deity of Christ, justification by faith, and many others would rightly be considered major doctrines. People who disagree with the historic evangelical understanding of any of these doctrines will have wide areas of difference with evangelical Christians who affirm these doctrines. By contrast, it seems to me that differences over forms of church government or some details about the Lord's Supper or the timing of the great tribulation concern minor doctrines. Christians who differ over these things can agree on perhaps every other area of doctrine, can live Christian lives that differ in no important way, and can have genuine fellowship with one another.

Of course, we may find doctrines that fall somewhere between "major" and "minor" according to this standard. For example, Christians may differ over the degree of significance that should attach to the doctrine of baptism or the millennium or the extent of the atonement. That is only natural, because many doctrines have *some* influence on other doctrines or on life, but we may differ over whether we think it to be a "significant" influence. We could even recognize that there will be a range of significance here and just say that the more influence a doctrine has on other doctrines and on life, the more "major" it becomes. This amount of influence may even vary according to the historical circumstances and needs of the church at any given time. In such cases, Christians will need to ask God to give them mature wisdom and sound judgment as they try to determine to what extent a doctrine should be considered "major" in their particular circumstances.

### D. A Note on Two Objections to the Study of Systematic Theology

**1. "The Conclusions Are 'Too Neat' to be True."** Some scholars look with suspicion at systematic theology when — or even because — its teachings fit together in a noncontradictory way. They object that the results are "too neat" and that systematic theologians must therefore be squeezing the Bible's teachings into an artificial mold, distorting the true meaning of Scripture to get an orderly set of beliefs.

To this objection two responses can be made: (1) We must first ask the people making the objection to tell us at what specific points Scripture has been misinterpreted, and then we must deal with the understanding of those passages. Perhaps mistakes have been made, and in that case there should be corrections.

Yet it is also possible that the objector will have no specific passages in mind, or no clearly erroneous interpretations to point to in the works of the most responsible evangelical theologians. Of course, incompetent exegesis can be found in the writings of the less competent scholars in *any* field of biblical studies, not just in systematic theology, but those "bad examples" constitute an objection not against the scholar's field but against the incompetent scholar himself.

It is very important that the objector be specific at this point because this objection is sometimes made by those who — perhaps unconsciously — have adopted from our culture a skeptical view of the possibility of finding universally true conclusions about anything, even about God from his Word. This kind of skepticism regarding theological truth is especially common in the modern university world where "systematic theology" — if it is studied at all — is studied only from the perspectives of philosophical theology and historical theology (including perhaps a historical study of the various ideas that were believed by the early Christians who wrote the New Testament, and by other Christians at that time and throughout church history). In this kind of intellectual climate the study of "systematic theology" as defined in this chapter would be considered impossible, because the Bible would be assumed to be merely the work of many human authors who wrote out of diverse cultures and experiences over the course of more than one thousand years: trying to find "what the whole Bible teaches" about any subject would be thought nearly as hopeless as trying to find "what all philosophers teach" about some question, for the answer in both cases would be thought to be not one view but many diverse and often conflicting views. This skeptical viewpoint must be rejected by evangelicals who see Scripture as the product of human *and* divine authorship, and therefore as a collection of writings that teach noncontradictory truths about God and about the universe he created.

(2) Second, it must be answered that in God's own mind, and in the nature of reality itself, *true* facts and ideas are all consistent with one another. Therefore if we have accurately understood the teachings of God in Scripture we should expect our conclusions to "fit together" and be mutually consistent. Internal consistency, then, is an argument for, not against, any individual results of systematic theology.

**2. "The Choice of Topics Dictates the Conclusions."** Another general objection to systematic theology concerns the choice and arrangement of topics, and even the fact that such topically arranged study of Scripture, using categories sometimes different from those found in Scripture itself, is done at all. Why are *these* theological topics treated rather than just the topics emphasized by the biblical authors, and why are the topics *arranged in this way* rather than in some other way? Perhaps — this objection would say — our traditions and our cultures have determined the topics we treat and the arrangement of topics, so that the results of this systematic-theological study of Scripture, though acceptable in our own theological tradition, will in fact be untrue to Scripture itself.

A variant of this objection is the statement that our starting point often determines our conclusions on controversial topics: if we decide to start with an emphasis on the divine authorship of Scripture, for example, we will end up believing in biblical inerrancy, but if we start with an emphasis on the human authorship of Scripture, we will end up believing there are some errors in the Bible. Similarly, if we start with an emphasis on God's sovereignty, we will end up as Calvinists, but if we start with an emphasis on man's ability to make free choices, we will end up as Arminians, and so forth. This objection makes it sound as if the most important theological questions could probably be decided by flipping a coin to decide where to start, since *different* and *equally valid* conclusions will inevitably be reached from the different starting points.

Those who make such an objection often suggest that the best way to avoid this problem is not to study or teach systematic theology at all, but to limit our topical studies to the field of biblical theology, treating only the topics and themes the biblical authors themselves emphasize and describing the historical development of these biblical themes through the Bible.

In response to this objection, much of the discussion in this chapter about the necessity to teach Scripture will be relevant. Our choice of topics need not be restricted to the main concerns of the biblical authors, for our goal is to find out what God requires of us in all areas of concern to us today.

For example, it was not the *main* concern of any New Testament author to explain such topics as "baptism in the Holy Spirit," or women's roles in the church, or the doctrine of the Trinity, but these are valid areas of concern for us today, and we must look at all the places in Scripture that have relevance for those topics (whether those specific terms are mentioned or not, and whether those themes are of primary concern to each passage we examine or not) if we are going to be able to understand and explain to others "what the whole Bible teaches" about them.

The only alternative—for we *will* think *something* about those subjects—is to form our opinions haphazardly from a general impression of what we feel to be a "biblical" position on each subject, or perhaps to buttress our positions with careful analysis of one or two relevant texts, yet with no guarantee that those texts present a balanced view of "the whole counsel of God" (Acts 20:27) on the subject being considered. In fact this approach—one all too common in evangelical circles today—could, I suppose, be called "unsystematic theology" or even "disorderly and random theology"! Such an alternative is too subjective and too subject to cultural pressures. It tends toward doctrinal fragmentation and wide-spread doctrinal uncertainty, leaving the church theologically immature, like "children, tossed to and fro and carried about with every wind of doctrine" (Eph. 4:14).

Concerning the objection about the choice and sequence of topics, there is nothing to prevent us from going to Scripture to look for answers to *any* doctrinal questions, considered in *any sequence*. The sequence of topics in this book is a very common one and has been adopted because it is orderly and lends itself well to learning and teaching. But the chapters could be read in any sequence one wanted and the conclusions should not be different, nor should the persuasiveness of the arguments—if they are rightly derived from Scripture—be significantly diminished. I have tried to write the chapters so that they can be read as independent units.

### E. How Should Christians Study Systematic Theology?

How then should we study systematic theology? The Bible provides some guidelines for answering this question.

**1. We Should Study Systematic Theology With Prayer.** If studying systematic theology is simply a certain way of studying the Bible, then the passages in Scripture that talk about the way in which we should study God's Word give guidance to us in this task. Just as the psalmist prays in Psalm 119:18, "Open my eyes, that I may behold wondrous things out of your law," so we should pray and seek God's help in understanding his Word. Paul tells us in 1 Corinthians 2:14 that "the unspiritual man does not receive the gifts of the Spirit of God, for they are folly to him, and he is not able to understand them because they are spiritually discerned." Studying theology is therefore a spiritual activity in which we need the help of the Holy Spirit.

No matter how intelligent, if the student does not continue to pray for God to give him or her an understanding mind and a believing and humble heart, and the student does not maintain a personal walk with the Lord, then the teachings of Scripture will be misunderstood and disbelieved, doctrinal error will result, and the mind and heart of the student will not be changed for the better but for the worse. Students of systematic theology should resolve at the beginning to keep their lives free from any disobedience to God or any known sin that would disrupt their relationship with him. They should resolve to maintain with great regularity their own personal devotional lives. They should continually pray for wisdom and understanding of Scripture.

Since it is the Holy Spirit who gives us the ability rightly to understand Scripture, we need to realize that the proper thing to do, particularly when we are unable to understand some passage or some doctrine of Scripture, is to pray for God's help. Often what we need is not more data but more insight into the data we already have available. This insight is given only by the Holy Spirit (cf. 1 Cor. 2:14; Eph. 1:17–19).

**2. We Should Study Systematic Theology With Humility.** Peter tells us, "Clothe yourselves, all of you, with humility toward one another, for 'God opposes the proud, but gives grace to the humble'" (1 Peter 5:5). Those who study systematic theology will learn many things about the teachings of Scripture that are perhaps not known or not known well by other Christians in their churches or by relatives who are older in the Lord than they are. They may also find that they understand things about Scripture that some of their church officers do not understand, and that even their pastor has perhaps forgotten or never learned well.

In all of these situations it would be very easy to adopt an attitude of pride or superiority toward others who have not made such a study. But how ugly it would be if anyone were to use this knowledge of God's Word simply to win arguments or to put down a fellow Christian in conversation, or to make another believer feel insignificant in the Lord's work. James' counsel is good for us at this point: "Let every man be quick to hear, slow to speak, slow to anger, for the anger of man does not work the righteousness of God" (James 1:19–20). He tells us that one's understanding of Scripture is to be imparted in humility and love:

> Who is wise and understanding among you? By his good life let him show his works in the meekness of wisdom. . . . But the wisdom from above is first pure, then peaceable, gentle, open to reason, full of mercy and good fruits, without uncertainty or insincerity. And the harvest of righteousness is sown in peace by those who make peace. (James 3:13, 17–18)

Systematic theology rightly studied will not lead to the knowledge that "puffs up" (1 Cor. 8:1) but to humility and love for others.

**3. We Should Study Systematic Theology With Reason.** We find in the New Testament that Jesus and the New Testament authors will often quote a verse of Scripture and then draw logical conclusions from it. They *reason* from Scripture. It is therefore not wrong to use human understanding, human logic, and human reason to draw conclusions from the statements of Scripture. Nevertheless, when we reason and draw what we think to be correct logical deductions from Scripture, we sometimes make mistakes. The deductions we draw from the statements of Scripture are not equal to the statements of Scripture themselves in certainty or authority, for our ability to reason and draw conclusions is not the ultimate standard of truth—only Scripture is.

What then are the limits on our use of our reasoning abilities to draw deductions from the statements of Scripture? The fact that reasoning to conclusions that go beyond the mere statements of Scripture is appropriate and even necessary for studying Scripture, and the fact that Scripture itself is the ultimate standard of truth, combine to indicate to us that *we are free to use our reasoning abilities to draw deductions from any passage of Scripture so long as these deductions do not contradict the clear teaching of some other passage of Scripture.*[7]

This principle puts a safeguard on our use of what we think to be logical deductions from Scripture. Our supposedly logical deductions may be erroneous, but Scripture itself cannot be erroneous. Thus, for example, we may read Scripture and find that God the Father is called God (1 Cor. 1:3), that God the Son is called God (John 20:28; Titus 2:13), and that God the Holy Spirit is called God (Acts 5:3–4). We might deduce from this that there are three Gods. But then we find the Bible explicitly teaching us that God is one (Deut. 6:4; James 2:19). Thus we conclude that what we *thought* to be a valid logical deduction about three Gods was wrong and that Scripture teaches both (a) that there are three separate persons (the Father, the Son, and the Holy Spirit), each of whom is fully God, and (b) that there is one God.

We cannot understand exactly how these two statements can both be true, so together they constitute a *paradox* ("a seemingly contradictory statement that may nonetheless be true").[8] We can tolerate a paradox (such as "God is three persons and one God") because we have confidence that ultimately God knows fully the truth about himself and about the nature of reality, and that in his understanding the different elements of a paradox are fully reconciled, even though at this point God's thoughts are higher than our thoughts (Isa. 55:8–9). But a true contradiction (such as, "God is three persons and God is not three persons") would imply ultimate contradiction in God's own understanding of himself or of reality, and this cannot be.

---

[7]This guideline is also adopted from Professor John Frame at Westminster Seminary.

[8]The *American Heritage Dictionary of the English Language,* ed. William Morris (Boston: Houghton-Mifflin, 1980), p. 950 (first definition). Essentially the same meaning is adopted by the *Oxford English Dictionary* (1913 ed., 7:450), the *Concise Oxford Dictionary* (1981 ed., p. 742), the *Random House College Dictionary* (1979 ed., p. 964), and the *Chambers Twentieth Century Dictionary* (p. 780), though all note that *paradox* can also mean "contradiction" (though less commonly); compare the *Encyclopedia of Philosophy,* ed. Paul Edwards (New York: Macmillan and The Free Press, 1967), 5:45, and the entire article "Logical Paradoxes" by John van Heijenoort on pp. 45–51 of the same volume, which proposes solutions to many of the classical paradoxes in the history of philosophy. (If *paradox* meant "contradiction," such solutions would be impossible.)

When I use the word *paradox* in the primary sense defined by these dictionaries today I realize that I am differing somewhat with the article "Paradox" by K. S. Kantzer in the *EDT,* ed. Walter Elwell, pp. 826–27 (which takes *paradox* to mean essentially "contradiction"). However, I am using *paradox* in an ordinary English sense and one also familiar in philosophy. There seems to me to be available no better word than *paradox* to refer to an apparent but not real contradiction.

There is, however, some lack of uniformity in the use of the term *paradox* and a related term, *antinomy,* in con-

temporary evangelical discussion. The word *antinomy* has sometimes been used to apply to what I here call *paradox,* that is, "seemingly contradictory statements that may nonetheless both be true" (see, for example, John Jefferson Davis, *Theology Primer* [Grand Rapids: Baker, 1981], p. 18). Such a sense for *antinomy* gained support in a widely read book, *Evangelism and the Sovereignty of God,* by J. I. Packer (London: Inter-Varsity Press, 1961). On pp. 18–22 Packer defines *antinomy* as "an appearance of contradiction" (but admits on p. 18 that his definition differs with the *Shorter Oxford Dictionary*). My problem with using *antinomy* in this sense is that the word is so unfamiliar in ordinary English that it just increases the stock of technical terms Christians have to learn in order to understand theologians, and moreover such a sense is unsupported by any of the dictionaries cited above, all of which define *antinomy* to mean "contradiction" (e.g., *Oxford English Dictionary,* 1:371). The problem is not serious, but it would help communication if evangelicals could agree on uniform senses for these terms.

A paradox is certainly acceptable in systematic theology, and paradoxes are in fact inevitable so long as we have finite understanding of any theological topic. However, it is important to recognize that Christian theology should never affirm a *contradiction* (a set of two statements, one of which denies the other). A contradiction would be, "God is three persons and God is not three persons" (where the term *persons* has the same sense in both halves of the sentence).

When the psalmist says, "The sum of your word is truth; and every one of your righteous ordinances endures for ever" (Ps. 119:160), he implies that God's words are not only true individually but also viewed together as a whole. Viewed collectively, their "sum" is also "truth." Ultimately, there is no internal contradiction either in Scripture or in God's own thoughts.

**4. We Should Study Systematic Theology With Help From Others.** We need to be thankful that God has put teachers in the church ("And God has appointed in the church first apostles, second prophets, third *teachers . . .*" [1 Cor. 12:28]. We should allow those with gifts of teaching to help us understand Scripture. This means that we should make use of systematic theologies and other books that have been written by some of the teachers that God has given to the church over the course of its history. It also means that our study of theology should include *talking with other Christians* about the things we study. Among those with whom we talk will often be some with gifts of teaching who can explain biblical teachings clearly and help us to understand more easily. In fact, some of the most effective learning in systematic theology courses in colleges and seminaries often occurs outside the classroom in informal conversations among students who are attempting to understand Bible doctrines for themselves.

**5. We Should Study Systematic Theology by Collecting and Understanding All the Relevant Passages of Scripture on Any Topic.** This point was mentioned in our definition of systematic theology at the beginning of the chapter, but the actual process needs to be described here. How does one go about making a doctrinal summary of what all the passages of Scripture teach on a certain topic? For topics covered in this book, many people will think that studying the chapters in this book and reading the Bible verses noted in the chapters is enough. But some people will want to do further study of Scripture on a particular topic or study some new topic not covered here. How could a student go about using the Bible to research its teachings on some new subject, perhaps one not discussed explicitly in any of his or her systematic theology textbooks?

The process would look like this: (1) Find all the relevant verses. The best help in this step is a good concordance, which enables one to look up key words and find the verses in which the subject is treated. For example, in studying what it means that man is created in the image and likeness of God, one needs to find all the verses in which "image" and "likeness" and "create" occur. (The words "man" and "God" occur too often to be useful for a concordance search.) In studying the doctrine of prayer, many words could be looked up (*pray, prayer, intercede, petition, supplication, confess, confession, praise, thanks, thanksgiving,* et al.) — and perhaps the list of verses would grow too long to be manageable, so that the student would have to skim the concordance entries without looking up the verses, or the search would probably have to be divided into sections or limited in some other way. Verses can also be found by thinking through the overall history of the Bible and then turning to sections where there would be information on the topic at hand — for example, a student studying prayer would want to read passages like the one about Hannah's prayer for a son (in 1 Sam. 1), Solomon's prayer at the dedication of the temple (in 1 Kings 8), Jesus' prayer in the Garden of Gethsemane (in Matt. 26 and parallels), and so forth. Then in addition to concordance work and reading other passages that one can find on the subject, checking the relevant sections in some systematic theology books will often bring to light other verses that had been missed, sometimes because none of the key words used for the concordance were in those verses.[9]

(2) The second step is to read, make notes on, and try to summarize the points made in the relevant verses. Sometimes a theme will be repeated often and the summary of the various verses will be relatively easy. At other times, there will be verses difficult to understand, and the student will need to take some time to study a verse in depth (just by reading the verse in context over and over, or by using specialized tools such as commentaries and dictionaries) until a satisfactory understanding is reached.

(3) Finally, the teachings of the various verses should be summarized into one or more points that the Bible affirms about that subject. The summary does not have to take the exact form of anyone else's conclusions on the subject, because we each may see things in Scripture that others have missed, or we may organize the subject differently or emphasize different things.

On the other hand, at this point it is also helpful to read related sections, if any can be found, in several systematic theology books. This provides a useful check against error and oversight, and often makes one aware of alternative perspectives and arguments that may cause us to modify or strengthen our position. If a student finds that others have argued for strongly differing conclusions, then these other views need to be stated fairly and then answered. Sometimes other theology books will alert us to historical or philosophical considerations that have been raised before in the history of the church, and these will provide additional insight or warnings against error.

The process outlined above is possible for any Christian who can read his or her Bible and can look up words in a concordance. Of course people will become faster and more accurate in this process with time and experience and Christian maturity, but it would be a tremendous help to the church if Christians generally would give much more time to searching out topics in Scripture for themselves and drawing conclusions in the way outlined above. The joy of discovery of biblical themes would be richly rewarding. Especially pastors and those who lead Bible studies would find added freshness in their understanding of Scripture and in their teaching.

**6. We Should Study Systematic Theology With Rejoicing and Praise.** The study of theology is not merely a theoretical exercise of the intellect. It is a study of the living God, and of the wonders of all his works in creation and redemption. We cannot study this subject dispassionately! We must love all that God is, all that he says and all that he does. "You shall love the LORD your God with all your heart" (Deut. 6:5). Our response to the study of the theology of Scripture should be that of the psalmist who said, "How precious to me are your thoughts, O God!" (Ps. 139:17). In the study of the teachings of

---

[9]I have read a number of student papers telling me that John's gospel says nothing about how Christians should pray, for example, because they looked at a concordance and found that the word *prayer* was not in John, and the word *pray* only occurs four times in reference to Jesus praying in John 14, 16, and 17. They overlooked the fact that John contains several important verses where the word *ask* rather than the word *pray* is used (John 14:13–14; 15:7, 16, et al.).

God's Word, it should not surprise us if we often find our hearts spontaneously breaking forth in expressions of praise and delight like those of the psalmist:

> The precepts of the LORD are right,
>     rejoicing the heart. (Ps. 19:8)

> In the way of your testimonies I delight
>     as much as in all riches. (Ps. 119:14)

> How sweet are your words to my taste,
>     sweeter than honey to my mouth! (Ps. 119:103)

> Your testimonies are my heritage for ever;
>     yea, they are the joy of my heart. (Ps. 119:111)

> I rejoice at your word
>     like one who finds great spoil. (Ps. 119:162)

Often in the study of theology the response of the Christian should be similar to that of Paul in reflecting on the long theological argument that he has just completed at the end of Romans 11:32. He breaks forth into joyful praise at the richness of the doctrine which God has enabled him to express:

> O the depth of the riches and wisdom and knowledge of God! How unsearchable are his judgments and how inscrutable his ways!

> "For who has known the mind of the Lord,
> or who has been his counselor?"
> "Or who has given a gift to him
> that he might be repaid?"

> For from him and through him and to him are all things. To him be glory for ever. Amen. (Rom. 11:33–36)

## QUESTIONS FOR PERSONAL APPLICATION

These questions at the end of each chapter focus on application to life. Because I think doctrine is to be felt at the emotional level as well as understood at the intellectual level, in many chapters I have included some questions about how a reader *feels* regarding a point of doctrine. I think these questions will prove quite valuable for those who take the time to reflect on them.

1. In what ways (if any) has this chapter changed your understanding of what systematic theology is? What was your attitude toward the study of systematic theology before reading this chapter? What is your attitude now?

2. What is likely to happen to a church or denomination that gives up learning systematic theology for a generation or longer? Has that been true of your church?

3. Are there any doctrines listed in the Contents for which a fuller understanding would help to solve a personal difficulty in your life at the present time? What

are the spiritual and emotional dangers that you personally need to be aware of in studying systematic theology?

4. Pray for God to make this study of basic Christian doctrines a time of spiritual growth and deeper fellowship with him, and a time in which you understand and apply the teachings of Scripture rightly.

## SPECIAL TERMS

| | |
|---|---|
| apologetics | minor doctrine |
| biblical theology | New Testament theology |
| Christian ethics | Old Testament theology |
| contradiction | paradox |
| doctrine | philosophical theology |
| dogmatic theology | presupposition |
| historical theology | systematic theology |
| major doctrine | |

## BIBLIOGRAPHY

Baker, D. L. "Biblical Theology." In *NDT*, p. 671.

Berkhof, Louis. *Introduction to Systematic Theology*. Grand Rapids: Eerdmans, 1982, pp. 15–75 (first published 1932).

Bray, Gerald L., ed. *Contours of Christian Theology*. Downers Grove, Ill.: InterVarsity Press, 1993.

_____. "Systematic Theology, History of." In *NDT*, pp. 671–72.

Cameron, Nigel M., ed. *The Challenge of Evangelical Theology: Essays in Approach and Method*. Edinburgh: Rutherford House, 1987.

Carson, D. A. "Unity and Diversity in the New Testament: The Possibility of Systematic Theology." In *Scripture and Truth*. Ed. by D. A. Carson and John Woodbridge. Grand Rapids: Zondervan, 1983, pp. 65–95.

Davis, John Jefferson. *Foundations of Evangelical Theology*. Grand Rapids: Baker, 1984.

_____. *The Necessity of Systematic Theology*. Grand Rapids: Baker, 1980.

_____. *Theology Primer: Resources for the Theological Student*. Grand Rapids: Baker, 1981.

Demarest, Bruce. "Systematic Theology." In *EDT*, pp. 1064–66.

Erickson, Millard. *Concise Dictionary of Christian Theology*. Grand Rapids: Baker, 1986.

Frame, John. *Van Til the Theologian*. Phillipsburg, N.J.: Pilgrim, 1976.

Geehan, E. R., ed. *Jerusalem and Athens*. Nutley, N.J.: Craig Press, 1971.

Grenz, Stanley J. *Revisioning Evangelical Theology: A Fresh Agenda for the 21st Century*. Downers Grove, Ill.: InterVarsity Press, 1993.

House, H. Wayne. *Charts of Christian Theology and Doctrine*. Grand Rapids: Zondervan, 1992.

Kuyper, Abraham. *Principles of Sacred Theology*. Trans. by J. H. DeVries. Grand Rapids: Eerdmans, 1968 (reprint; first published as *Encyclopedia of Sacred Theology* in 1898).

Machen, J. Gresham. *Christianity and Liberalism.* Grand Rapids: Eerdmans, 1923. (This 180-page book is, in my opinion, one of the most significant theological studies ever written. It gives a clear overview of major biblical doctrines and shows the vital differences with Protestant liberal theology at every point, differences that still confront us today. It is required reading in all my introductory theology classes.)

Morrow, T. W. "Systematic Theology." In *NDT,* p. 671.

Poythress, Vern. *Symphonic Theology: The Validity of Multiple Perspectives in Theology.* Grand Rapids: Zondervan, 1987.

Preus, Robert D. *The Theology of Post-Reformation Lutheranism: A Study of Theological Prolegomena.* 2 vols. St. Louis: Concordia, 1970.

Van Til, Cornelius. *In Defense of the Faith,* vol. 5: *An Introduction to Systematic Theology.* N.p.: Presbyterian and Reformed, 1976, pp. 1–61, 253–62.

_____. *The Defense of the Faith.* Philadelphia: Presbyterian and Reformed, 1955.

Vos, Geerhardus. "The Idea of Biblical Theology as a Science and as a Theological Discipline." In *Redemptive History and Biblical Interpretation,* pp. 3–24. Ed. by Richard Gaffin. Phillipsburg, N.J.: Presbyterian and Reformed, 1980 (article first published 1894).

Warfield, B. B. "The Indispensableness of Systematic Theology to the Preacher." In *Selected Shorter Writings of Benjamin B. Warfield,* 2:280–88. Ed. by John E. Meeter. Nutley, N.J.: Presbyterian and Reformed, 1973 (article first published 1897).

_____. "The Right of Systematic Theology." In *Selected Shorter Writings of Benjamin B. Warfield,* 2:21–279. Ed. by John E. Meeter. Nutley, N.J.: Presbyterian and Reformed, 1973 (article first published 1896).

Wells, David. *No Place for Truth, or, Whatever Happened to Evangelical Theology?* Grand Rapids: Eerdmans, 1993.

Woodbridge, John D., and Thomas E. McComiskey, eds. *Doing Theology in Today's World: Essays in Honor of Kenneth S. Kantzer.* Grand Rapids: Zondervan, 1991.

# SCRIPTURE MEMORY PASSAGE

Students have repeatedly mentioned that one of the most valuable parts of any of their courses in college or seminary has been the Scripture passages they were required to memorize. "I have hidden your word in my heart that I might not sin against you" (Ps. 119:11 NIV). In each chapter, therefore, I have included an appropriate memory passage so that instructors may incorporate Scripture memory into the course requirements wherever possible. (Scripture memory passages at the end of each chapter are taken from the RSV. These same passages in the NIV and NASB may be found in appendix 2.)

**Matthew 28:18–20:** *And Jesus came and said to them, "All authority in heaven and on earth has been given to me. Go therefore and make disciples of all nations, baptizing them in the name of the Father and of the Son and of the Holy Spirit, teaching them to observe all that I have commanded you; and lo, I am with you always, to the close of the age."*

## HYMN

Systematic theology at its best will result in praise. It is appropriate therefore at the end of each chapter to include a hymn related to the subject of that chapter. In a classroom setting, the hymn can be sung together at the beginning or end of class. Alternatively, an individual reader can sing it privately or simply meditate quietly on the words.

For almost every chapter the words of the hymns were found in *Trinity Hymnal* (Philadelphia: Great Commission Publications, 1990),[10] the hymnal of the Presbyterian Church in America and the Orthodox Presbyterian Church, but most of them are found in many other common hymnals. Unless otherwise noted, the words of these hymns are now in public domain and no longer subject to copyright restrictions: therefore they may be freely copied for overhead projector use or photocopied.

Why have I used so many old hymns? Although I personally like many of the more recent worship songs that have come into wide use, when I began to select hymns that would correspond to the great doctrines of the Christian faith, I realized that the great hymns of the church throughout history have a doctrinal richness and breadth that is still unequaled. For several of the chapters in this book, I know of no modern worship song that covers the same subject in an extended way—perhaps this can be a challenge to modern songwriters to study these chapters and then write songs reflecting the teaching of Scripture on the respective subjects.

For this chapter, however, I found no hymn ancient or modern that thanked God for the privilege of studying systematic theology from the pages of Scripture. Therefore I have selected a hymn of general praise, which is always appropriate.

### "O for a Thousand Tongues to Sing"

This hymn by Charles Wesley (1707–88) begins by wishing for "a thousand tongues" to sing God's praise. Verse 2 is a prayer that God would "assist me" in singing his praise throughout the earth. The remaining verses give praise to Jesus (vv. 3–6) and to God the Father (v. 7).

O for a thousand tongues to sing
My great Redeemer's praise,
The glories of my God and King,
The triumphs of His grace.

My gracious Master and my God,
Assist me to proclaim,
To spread through all the earth abroad,
The honors of Thy name.

Jesus! the name that charms our fears,
That bids our sorrows cease;

---

[10]This hymn book is completely revised from a similar hymnal of the same title published by the Orthodox Presbyterian Church in WW 1961.

'Tis music in the sinner's ears,
'Tis life and health and peace.

He breaks the pow'r of reigning sin,
He sets the prisoner free;
His blood can make the foulest clean;
His blood availed for me.

He speaks and, list'ning to His voice,
New life the dead receive;
The mournful, broken hearts rejoice;
The humble poor believe.

Hear him, ye deaf; his praise, ye dumb,
Your loosened tongues employ,
Ye blind, behold your Savior come;
And leap, ye lame, for joy.

Glory to God and praise and love
Be ever, ever giv'n
By saints below and saints above—
The church in earth and heav'n.

AUTHOR: CHARLES WESLEY, 1739, ALT.

# Chapter 2

# THE WORD OF GOD

## *What are the different forms of the Word of God?*

## EXPLANATION AND SCRIPTURAL BASIS

What is meant by the phrase "the Word of God"? Actually, there are several different meanings taken by this phrase in the Bible. It is helpful to distinguish these different senses clearly at the beginning of this study.

### A. "The Word of God" as a Person: Jesus Christ

Sometimes the Bible refers to the Son of God as "the Word of God." In Revelation 19:13, John sees the risen Lord Jesus in heaven and says, "The name by which he is called is The Word of God." Similarly, in the beginning of John's gospel we read, "In the beginning was the Word, and the Word was with God, and the Word was God" (John 1:1). It is clear that John is speaking of the Son of God here, because in verse 14 he says, "And the Word became flesh and dwelt among us, full of grace and truth; we have beheld his glory, glory as of the only Son from the Father." These verses (and perhaps 1 John 1:1) are the only instances where the Bible refers to God the Son as "the Word" or "the Word of God," so this usage is not common. But it does indicate that among the members of the Trinity it is especially God the Son who in his person as well as in his words has the role of communicating the character of God to us and of expressing the will of God for us.

### B. "The Word of God" as Speech by God

**1. God's Decrees.** Sometimes God's words take the form of powerful decrees that cause events to happen or even cause things to come into being. "And God said, 'Let there be light'; and there was light" (Gen. 1:3). God even created the animal world by speaking his powerful word: "And God said, 'Let the earth bring forth living creatures according to their kinds: cattle and creeping things and beasts of the earth according to their kinds.' And it was so" (Gen. 1:24). Thus, the psalmist can say, "*By the word of the Lord* the heavens were made, and all their host by the breath of his mouth" (Ps. 33:6).

These powerful, creative words from God are often called God's decrees. A *decree* of God is a word of God that causes something to happen. These decrees of God include not only the events of the original creation but also the continuing existence of all things, for Hebrews 1:3 tells us that Christ is continually "upholding the universe by his word of power."

**2. God's Words of Personal Address.** God sometimes communicates with people on earth by speaking directly to them. These can be called instances of God's Word of *personal address.* Examples are found throughout Scripture. At the very beginning of creation God speaks to Adam: "And the LORD God commanded the man, saying, 'You may freely eat of every tree of the garden; but of the tree of the knowledge of good and evil you shall not eat, for in the day that you eat of it you shall die'" (Gen. 2:16–17). After the sin of Adam and Eve, God still comes and speaks directly and personally to them in the words of the curse (Gen. 3:16–19). Another prominent example of God's direct personal address to people on earth is found in the giving of the Ten Commandments: "And *God spoke all these words,* saying, 'I am the LORD your God, who brought you out of the land of Egypt, out of the house of bondage. You shall have no other gods before me . . .'" (Ex. 20:1–3). In the New Testament, at Jesus' baptism, God the Father spoke with a voice from heaven, saying, "This is my beloved Son, with whom I am well pleased" (Matt. 3:17).

In these and several other instances where God spoke words of personal address to individual people it was clear to the hearers that these were the actual words of God: they were hearing God's very voice, and they were therefore hearing words that had absolute divine authority and that were absolutely trustworthy. To disbelieve or disobey any of these words would have been to disbelieve or disobey God and therefore would have been sin.

Though the words of God's personal address are always seen in Scripture to be the actual words of God, they are *also "human" words* in that they are spoken in ordinary human language that is immediately understandable. The fact that these words are spoken in human language does not limit their divine character or authority in any way: they are still entirely the words of God, spoken by the voice of God himself.

Some theologians have argued that since human language is always in some sense "imperfect," any message that God addresses to us in human language must also be limited in its authority or truthfulness. But these passages and many others that record instances of God's words of personal address to individuals give no indication of any limitation of the authority or truthfulness of God's words when they are spoken in human language. Quite the contrary is true, for the words always place an absolute obligation upon the hearers to believe them and to obey them fully. To disbelieve or disobey any part of them is to disbelieve or disobey God himself.

**3. God's Words as Speech Through Human Lips.** Frequently in Scripture God raises up prophets through whom he speaks. Once again, it is evident that although these are human words, spoken in ordinary human language by ordinary human beings, the authority and truthfulness of these words is in no way diminished: they are still completely God's words as well.

In Deuteronomy 18, God says to Moses:

> I will raise up for them a prophet like you from among their brethren; and *I will put my words in his mouth,* and he shall speak to them all that I command him. And whoever will not give heed to my words which he shall speak in my name, I myself will require it of him. But the prophet who presumes to speak a word in my name which I have not commanded him to speak, or who speaks in the name of other gods, that same prophet shall die. (Deut. 18:18–20)

God made a similar statement to Jeremiah: "Then the Lord put forth his hand and touched my mouth; and the Lord said to me, 'Behold, *I have put my words in your mouth'"* (Jer. 1:9). God tells Jeremiah, "Whatever I command you you shall speak" (Jer. 1:7; see also Ex. 4:12; Num. 22:38; 1 Sam. 15:3, 18, 23; 1 Kings 20:36; 2 Chron. 20:20; 25:15–16; Isa. 30:12–14; Jer. 6:10–12; 36:29–31, et al.). Anyone who claimed to be speaking for the Lord but who had not received a message from him was severely punished (Ezek. 13:1–7; Deut. 18:20–22).

Thus God's words spoken through human lips were considered to be just as authoritative and just as true as God's words of personal address. There was no diminishing of the authority of these words when they were spoken through human lips. To disbelieve or disobey any of them was to disbelieve or disobey God himself.

**4. God's Words in Written Form (the Bible).** In addition to God's words of decree, God's words of personal address, and God's words spoken through the lips of human beings, we also find in Scripture several instances where God's words were put in *written form.* The first of these is found in the narrative of the giving of the two tablets of stone on which were written the Ten Commandments: "And he gave to Moses, when he had made an end of speaking with him upon Mount Sinai, the two tables of the testimony, tables of stone, *written with the finger of God"* (Ex. 31:18). "And the tables were the work of God, and *the writing was the writing of God, graven upon the tables"* (Ex. 32:16; 34:1, 28).

Further writing was done by Moses:

> *And Moses wrote this law,* and gave it to the priests the sons of Levi, who carried the ark of the covenant of the Lord, and to all the elders of Israel. And Moses commanded them, "At the end of every seven years . . . you shall read this law before all Israel in their hearing . . . that they may hear and learn to fear the Lord your God, and be careful to do all the words of this law, and that their children, who have not known it, may hear and learn to fear the Lord your God. . . ." (Deut. 31:9–13)

This book which Moses wrote was then deposited by the side of the ark of the covenant: "When Moses had finished *writing the words of this law in a book,* to the very end, Moses commanded the Levites who carried the ark of the covenant of the Lord, 'Take this book of the law, and put it by the side of the ark of the covenant of the Lord your God, that it may be there for a witness against you'" (Deut. 31:24–26).

Further additions were made to this book of God's words. "And *Joshua wrote these words* in the book of the law of God" (Josh. 24:26). God commanded Isaiah, "And now, go, *write it before them on a tablet, and inscribe it in a book,* that it may be for the time to come as a witness for ever" (Isa. 30:8). Once again, God said to Jeremiah, "*Write in a book* all the words that I have spoken to you" (Jer. 30:2; cf. Jer. 36:2–4, 27–31; 51:60). In the New Testament, Jesus promises his disciples that the Holy Spirit would bring to their remembrance the words which he, Jesus, had spoken (John 14:26; cf. 16:12–13). Paul can say that the very words he writes to the Corinthians are "a command of the Lord" (1 Cor. 14:37; cf. 2 Peter 3:2).

Once again it must be noted that these words are still considered to be God's own words, even though they are written down mostly by human beings and always in human language. Still, they are absolutely authoritative and absolutely true: to disobey them or disbelieve them is a serious sin and brings judgment from God (1 Cor. 14:37; Jer. 36:29–31).

Several benefits come from the writing down of God's words. First, there is a much *more accurate preservation* of God's words for subsequent generations. To depend on memory and the repeating of oral tradition is a less reliable method of preserving these words throughout history than is their recording in writing (cf. Deut. 31:12–13). Second, the *opportunity for repeated inspection* of words that are written down permits careful study and discussion, which leads to better understanding and more complete obedience. Third, God's words in writing are *accessible to many more people* than they are when preserved merely through memory and oral repetition. They can be inspected at any time by any person and are not limited in accessibility to those who have memorized them or those who are able to be present when they are recited orally. Thus, the reliability, permanence, and accessibility of the form in which God's words are preserved are all greatly enhanced when they are written down. Yet there is no indication that their authority or truthfulness is diminished.

## C. The Focus of Our Study

Of all the forms of the Word of God,[1] the focus of our study in systematic theology is God's Word in written form, that is, the Bible. This is the form of God's Word that is available for study, for public inspection, for repeated examination, and as a basis for mutual discussion. It tells us about and points us to the Word of God as a person, namely Jesus Christ, whom we do not now have present in bodily form on earth. Thus, we are no longer able to observe and imitate his life and teachings firsthand.

The other forms of the Word of God are not suitable as the primary basis for the study of theology. We do not hear God's words of decree and thus cannot study them directly but only through observation of their effects. God's words of personal address are uncommon, even in Scripture. Furthermore, even if we did hear some words of personal address from God to ourselves today, we would not have certainty that our understanding of it,

---

[1]In addition to the forms of God's Word mentioned above, God communicates to people through different types of "general revelation"—that is, revelation that is given not just to certain people but to all people generally. General revelation includes both the revelation of God that comes through nature (see Ps. 19:1–6; Acts 14:17) and the revelation of God that comes through the inner sense of right and wrong in every person's heart (Rom. 2:15). These kinds of revelation are nonverbal in form, and I have not included them in the list of various forms of the Word of God discussed in this chapter. (See chapter 7, Section E, for further discussion of general revelation.)

our memory of it, and our subsequent report of it was wholly accurate. Nor would we be readily able to convey to others the certainty that the communication was from God, even if it was. God's words as spoken through human lips ceased to be given when the New Testament canon was completed.[2] Thus, these other forms of God's words are inadequate as a primary basis for study in theology.

It is most profitable for us to study God's words as written in the Bible. It is God's written Word that he commands us to study. The man is "blessed" who "meditates" on God's law "day and night" (Ps. 1:1–2). God's words to Joshua are also applicable to us: "This book of the law shall not depart out of your mouth, but *you shall meditate on it day and night,* that you may be careful to do all that is written in it; for then you shall make your way prosperous, and then you shall have good success" (Josh. 1:8). It is the Word of God in the form of written Scripture that is "God-breathed" and "useful for teaching, rebuking, correcting, and training in righteousness" (2 Tim. 3:16 NIV).

## QUESTIONS FOR PERSONAL APPLICATION

1. Do you think you would pay more attention if God spoke to you from heaven or through the voice of a living prophet than if he spoke to you from the written words of Scripture? Would you believe or obey such words more readily than you do Scripture? Do you think your present level of response to the written words of Scripture is an appropriate one? What positive steps can you take to make your attitude toward Scripture more like the kind of attitude God wants you to have?

2. When you think about the many ways in which God speaks and the frequency with which God communicates with his creatures through these means, what conclusions might you draw concerning the nature of God and the things that bring delight to him?

## SPECIAL TERMS

decree                                          personal address
Word of God

## BIBLIOGRAPHY

Kline, Meredith. *The Structure of Biblical Authority.* Grand Rapids: Eerdmans, 1972.

Kuyper, Abraham. *Principles of Sacred Theology.* Trans. by J. H. de Vries. Grand Rapids: Eerdmans, 1968, pp. 405–12 (originally published as *Encyclopedia of Sacred Theology* in 1898).

McDonald, H. D. *Theories of Revelation: An Historical Study, 1860–1960.* Grand Rapids: Baker, 1979.

_____. "Word, Word of God, Word of the Lord." In *EDT,* pp. 1185–88.

Packer, J. I. "Scripture." In *NDT,* pp. 585–87.

---

[2]See chapter 3 on the canon of Scripture.

Pinnock, C. H. "Revelation." In *NDT*, pp. 585–87.

Vos, Geerhardus. *Biblical Theology: Old and New Testaments.* Grand Rapids: Eerdmans, 1948, pp. 28–55; 321–27.

## SCRIPTURE MEMORY PASSAGE

**Ps. 1:1–2:**    *Blessed is the man*
*who walks not in the counsel of the wicked,*
*nor stands in the way of sinners,*
*nor sits in the seat of scoffers;*
*but his delight is in the law of the Lord,*
*and on his law he meditates day and night.*

## HYMN

### "Break Thou the Bread of Life"

This hymn is a prayer asking the Lord to give us not physical bread but spiritual nourishment from the "bread of life," a metaphor referring both to the written Word of God ("the sacred page," v. 1) and to Christ himself, the "Living Word" (see vv. 1, 3).

Break thou the bread of life, dear Lord, to me,
As thou didst break the loaves beside the sea;
Throughout the sacred page I seek thee, Lord,
My spirit pants for thee, O Living Word.

Bless thou the truth, dear Lord, to me, to me,
As thou didst bless the bread by Galilee;
Then shall all bondage cease, all fetters fall;
And I shall find my peace, my all in all.

Thou art the bread of life, O Lord, to me,
Thy holy Word the truth that saveth me;
Give me to eat and live with thee above;
Teach me to love thy truth, for thou art love.

O send thy Spirit, Lord, now unto me,
That he may touch mine eyes, and make me see:
Show me the truth concealed within thy Word,
And in thy Book revealed I see the Lord.

AUTHOR: MARY A. LATHBURY, 1877

# Chapter 3

# THE CANON OF SCRIPTURE

## *What belongs in the Bible and what does not belong?*

### EXPLANATION AND SCRIPTURAL BASIS

The previous chapter concluded that it is especially the written words of God in the Bible to which we are to give our attention. Before we can do this, however, we must know which writings belong in the Bible and which do not. This is the question of the canon of Scripture, which may be defined as follows: *The canon of Scripture is the list of all the books that belong in the Bible.*

We must not underestimate the importance of this question. The words of Scripture are the words by which we nourish our spiritual lives. Thus we can reaffirm the comment of Moses to the people of Israel in reference to the words of God's law: "For it is no trifle for you, but *it is your life,* and thereby you shall live long in the land which you are going over the Jordan to possess" (Deut. 32:47).

To add to or subtract from God's words would be to prevent God's people from obeying him fully, for commands that were subtracted would not be known to the people, and words that were added might require extra things of the people which God had not commanded. Thus Moses warned the people of Israel, "You shall not *add to the word* which I command you, *nor take from it;* that you may keep the commandments of the LORD your God which I command you" (Deut. 4:2).

The precise determination of the extent of the canon of Scripture is therefore of the utmost importance. If we are to trust and obey God absolutely we must have a collection of words that we are certain are God's own words to us. If there are any sections of Scripture about which we have doubts whether they are God's words or not, we will not consider them to have absolute divine authority and we will not trust them as much as we would trust God himself.

## A. The Old Testament Canon

Where did the idea of a canon begin—the idea that the people of Israel should preserve a collection of written words from God? Scripture itself bears witness to the historical development of the canon. The earliest collection of written words of God was the Ten Commandments. The Ten Commandments thus form the beginning of the biblical canon. God himself wrote on two tablets of stone the words which he commanded his people: "And he gave to Moses, when he had made an end of speaking with him upon Mount Sinai, the two tables of the testimony, tables of stone, *written with the finger of God*" (Ex. 31:18). Again we read, "And the tables were the work of God, and *the writing was the writing of God*, graven upon the tables" (Ex. 32:16; cf. Deut. 4:13; 10:4). The tablets were deposited in the ark of the covenant (Deut. 10:5) and constituted the terms of the covenant between God and his people.[1]

This collection of absolutely authoritative words from God grew in size throughout the time of Israel's history. Moses himself wrote additional words to be deposited beside the ark of the covenant (Deut. 31:24–26). The immediate reference is apparently to the book of Deuteronomy, but other references to writing by Moses indicate that the first four books of the Old Testament were written by him as well (see Ex. 17:14; 24:4; 34:27; Num. 33:2; Deut. 31:22). After the death of Moses, Joshua also added to the collection of written words of God: "Joshua wrote these words in the book of the law of God" (Josh. 24:26). This is especially surprising in light of the command not to add to or take away from the words which God gave the people through Moses: "You shall not add to the word which I command you, nor take from it . . ." (Deut. 4:2; cf. 12:32). In order to have disobeyed such a specific command, Joshua must have been convinced that he was not taking it upon himself to add to the written words of God, but that God himself had authorized such additional writing.

Later, others in Israel, usually those who fulfilled the office of prophet, wrote additional words from God:

> Samuel told the people the rights and duties of the kingship; and he wrote them in a book and laid it up before the LORD. (1 Sam. 10:25)

> The acts of King David, from first to last, are written in the Chronicles of Samuel the seer, and in the Chronicles of Nathan the prophet, and in the Chronicles of Gad the seer. (1 Chron. 29:29)

> Now the rest of the acts of Jehoshaphat, from first to last, are written in the chronicles of Jehu the son of Hanani, which are recorded in the Book of the Kings of Israel. (2 Chron. 20:34; cf. 1 Kings 16:7 where Jehu the son of Hanani is called a prophet)

> Now the rest of the acts of Uzziah, from first to last, Isaiah the prophet the son of Amoz wrote. (2 Chron. 26:22)

---

[1]See Meredith Kline, *The Structure of Biblical Authority* (Grand Rapids: Eerdmans, 1972), esp. pp. 48–53 and 113–30.

> Now the rest of the acts of Hezekiah, and his good deeds, behold, they are written in the vision of Isaiah the prophet the son of Amoz, in the Book of the Kings of Judah and Israel. (2 Chron. 32:32)

> Thus says the LORD, the God of Israel: Write in a book all the words that I have spoken to you.[2] (Jer. 30:2)

The content of the Old Testament canon continued to grow until the time of the end of the writing process. If we date Haggai to 520 B.C., Zechariah to 520–518 B.C. (with perhaps more material added after 480 B.C.), and Malachi around 435 B.C., we have an idea of the approximate dates of the last Old Testament prophets. Roughly coinciding with this period are the last books of Old Testament history—Ezra, Nehemiah, and Esther. Ezra went to Jerusalem in 458 B.C., and Nehemiah was in Jerusalem from 445–433 B.C.[3] Esther was written sometime after the death of Xerxes-I (= Ahasuerus) in 465 B.C., and a date during the reign of Artaxerxes I (464–423 B.C.) is probable. Thus, after approximately 435 B.C. there were no further additions to the Old Testament canon. The subsequent history of the Jewish people was recorded in other writings, such as the books of the Maccabees, but these writings were not thought worthy to be included with the collections of God's words from earlier years.

When we turn to Jewish literature outside the Old Testament, we see that the belief that divinely authoritative words from God had ceased is clearly attested in several different strands of extrabiblical Jewish literature. In 1 Maccabees (about 100 B.C.) the author writes of the defiled altar, "So they tore down the altar and stored the stones in a convenient place on the temple hill until there should come a prophet to tell what to do with them" (1 Macc. 4:45–46). They apparently knew of no one who could speak with the authority of God as the Old Testament prophets had done. The memory of an authoritative prophet among the people was one that belonged to the distant past, for the author could speak of a great distress "such as had not been since the time that prophets ceased to appear among them" (1 Macc. 9:27; cf. 14:41).

Josephus (born c. A.D. 37/38) explained, "From Artaxerxes to our own times a complete history has been written, but has not been deemed worthy of equal credit with the earlier records, because of the failure of the exact succession of the prophets" (*Against Apion* 1.41). This statement by the greatest Jewish historian of the first century A.D. shows that he knew of the writings now considered part of the "Apocrypha," but that he (and many of his contemporaries) considered these other writings "not . . . worthy of equal credit" with what we now know as the Old Testament Scriptures. There had been, in Josephus's viewpoint, no more "words of God" added to Scripture after about 435 B.C.

Rabbinic literature reflects a similar conviction in its repeated statement that the Holy Spirit (in the Spirit's function of inspiring prophecy) departed from Israel. "After the latter prophets Haggai, Zechariah, and Malachi had died, the Holy Spirit departed

---

[2]For other passages that illustrate the growth in the collection of written words from God see 2 Chron. 9:29; 12:15; 13:22; Isa. 30:8; Jer. 29:1; 36:1–32; 45:1; 51:60; Ezek. 43:11; Dan. 7:1; Hab. 2:2. Additions to it were usually through the agency of a prophet.

[3]See "Chronology of the Old Testament," in *IBD*, 1:277.

from Israel, but they still availed themselves of the *bath qôl*" (*Babylonian Talmud,* Yomah 9b, repeated in Sota 48b, Sanhedrin 11a, and Midrash Rabbah on Song of Songs, 8.9.3).[4]

The Qumran community (the Jewish sect that left behind the Dead Sea Scrolls) also awaited a prophet whose words would have authority to supersede any existing regulations (see 1 QS 9.11), and other similar statements are found elsewhere in ancient Jewish literature (see 2 Baruch 85.3 and Prayer of Azariah 15). Thus, writings subsequent to about 435 B.C. were not accepted by the Jewish people generally as having equal authority with the rest of Scripture.

In the New Testament, we have no record of any dispute between Jesus and the Jews over the extent of the canon. Apparently there was full agreement between Jesus and his disciples, on the one hand, and the Jewish leaders or Jewish people, on the other hand, that additions to the Old Testament canon had ceased after the time of Ezra, Nehemiah, Esther, Haggai, Zechariah, and Malachi. This fact is confirmed by the quotations of Jesus and the New Testament authors from the Old Testament. According to one count, Jesus and the New Testament authors quote various parts of the Old Testament Scriptures as divinely authoritative over 295 times,[5] but not once do they cite any statement from the books of the Apocrypha or any other writings as having divine authority.[6] The absence of any such reference to other literature as divinely authoritative, and the extremely frequent reference to hundreds of places in the Old Testament as divinely authoritative, gives strong confirmation to the fact that the New Testament authors agreed that the established Old Testament canon, no more and no less, was to be taken as God's very words.

What then shall be said about the Apocrypha, the collection of books included in the canon by the Roman Catholic Church but excluded from the canon by Protestantism?[7] These books were never accepted by the Jews as Scripture, but throughout the early history of the church there was a divided opinion on whether they should be part of Scripture or not. In fact, the earliest Christian evidence is decidedly against viewing the Apocrypha as Scripture, but the use of the Apocrypha gradually increased in some parts of the church until the time of the Reformation.[8] The fact that these books were

---

[4]That "the Holy Spirit" is primarily a reference to divinely authoritative prophecy is clear both from the fact that the *bath qôl* (a voice from heaven) is seen as a substitute for it, and from the very frequent use of "the Holy Spirit" to refer to prophecy elsewhere in Rabbinic literature.

[5]See Roger Nicole, "New Testament Use of the Old Testament," in *Revelation and the Bible,* ed. Carl F. H. Henry (London: Tyndale Press, 1959), pp. 137–41.

[6]Jude 14–15 does cite 1 Enoch 60.8 and 1.9, and Paul at least twice quotes pagan Greek authors (see Acts 17:28; Titus 1:12), but these citations are more for purposes of illustration than proof. Never are the works introduced with a phrase like, "God says," or "Scripture says," or "it is written," phrases that imply the attribution of divine authority to the words cited. (It should be noted that neither 1 Enoch nor the authors cited by Paul are part of the Apocrypha.) No book of the Apocrypha is even mentioned in the New Testament.

[7]The Apocrypha includes the following writings: 1 and 2 Esdras, Tobit, Judith, the Rest of Esther, the Wisdom of Solo-

mon, Ecclesiasticus, Baruch (including the Epistle of Jeremiah), the Song of the Three Holy Children, Susanna, Bel and the Dragon, the Prayer of Manasseh, and 1 and 2 Maccabees. These writings are not found in the Hebrew Bible, but they were included with the Septuagint (the translation of the Old Testament into Greek, which was used by many Greek-speaking Jews at the time of Christ). A good modern translation is *The Oxford Annotated Apocrypha (RSV),* ed. Bruce M. Metzger (New York: Oxford University Press, 1965). Metzger includes brief introductions and helpful annotations to the books.

The Greek word *apocrypha* means "things that are hidden," but Metzger notes (p. ix) that scholars are not sure why this word came to be applied to these writings.

[8]A detailed historical survey of the differing views of Christians regarding the Apocrypha is found in F. F. Bruce, *The Canon of Scripture* (Downers Grove, Ill.: InterVarsity Press, 1988), pp. 68–97. An even more detailed study is found in Roger Beckwith, *The Old Testament Canon of the New Testament Church and Its Background in Early Judaism* (London:

included by Jerome in his Latin Vulgate translation of the Bible (completed in A.D. 404) gave support to their inclusion, even though Jerome himself said they were not "books of the canon" but merely "books of the church" that were helpful and useful for believers. The wide use of the Latin Vulgate in subsequent centuries guaranteed their continued accessibility, but the fact that they had no Hebrew original behind them, and their exclusion from the Jewish canon, as well as the lack of their citation in the New Testament, led many to view them with suspicion or to reject their authority. For instance, the earliest Christian list of Old Testament books that exists today is by Melito, bishop of Sardis, writing about A.D. 170:[9]

> When I came to the east and reached the place where these things were preached and done, and learnt accurately the books of the Old Testament, I set down the facts and sent them to you. These are their names: five books of Moses, Genesis, Exodus, Numbers, Leviticus, Deuteronomy, Joshua the son of Nun, Judges, Ruth, four books of Kingdoms,[10] two books of Chronicles, the Psalms of David, the Proverbs of Solomon and his Wisdom,[11] Ecclesiastes, the Song of Songs, Job, the prophets Isaiah, Jeremiah, the Twelve in a single book, Daniel, Ezekiel, Ezra.[12]

It is noteworthy here that Melito names none of the books of the Apocrypha, but he includes all of our present Old Testament books except Esther.[13] Eusebius also quotes Origen as affirming most of the books of our present Old Testament canon (including Esther), but no book of the Apocrypha is affirmed as canonical, and the books of Maccabees are explicitly said to be "outside of these [canonical books]."[14] Similarly, in A.D. 367, when the great church leader Athanasius, bishop of Alexandria, wrote his Paschal Letter, he listed all the books of our present New Testament canon and all the books of our present Old Testament canon except Esther. He also mentioned some books of the Apocrypha such as the Wisdom of Solomon, the Wisdom of Sirach, Judith, and Tobit, and said these are "not indeed included in the Canon, but appointed by the Fathers

---

SPCK, 1985, and Grand Rapids: Eerdmans, 1986), esp. pp. 338–433. Beckwith's book has now established itself as the definitive work on the Old Testament canon. At the conclusion of his study Beckwith says, "The inclusion of various Apocrypha and Pseudepigrapha in the canon of the early Christians was not done in any agreed way or at the earliest period, but occurred in Gentile Christianity, after the church's breach with the synagogue, among those whose knowledge of the primitive Christian canon was becoming blurred." He concludes, "On the question of the canonicity of the Apocrypha and Pseudepigrapha the truly primitive Christian evidence is negative" (pp. 436–37).

[9]From Eusebius, *Ecclesiastical History* 4.26.14. Eusebius, writing in A.D. 325, was the first great church historian. This quotation is from the translation by Kirsopp Lake, *Eusebius: The Ecclesiastical History,* two vols. (London: Heinemann; and Cambridge, Mass.: Harvard, 1975), 1:393.

[10]That is, 1 Samuel, 2 Samuel, 1 Kings, and 2 Kings.

[11]This does not refer to the apocryphal book called the Wisdom of Solomon but is simply a fuller description of Proverbs. Eusebius notes in 4.22.9 that Proverbs was commonly called Wisdom by ancient writers.

[12]Ezra would include both Ezra and Nehemiah, according to a common Hebrew way of referring to the combined books.

[13]For some reason there was doubt about the canonicity of Esther in some parts of the early church (in the East but not in the West), but the doubts were eventually resolved, and Christian usage eventually became uniform with the Jewish view, which had always counted Esther as part of the canon, although it had been opposed by certain rabbis for their own reasons. (See the discussion of the Jewish view in Beckwith, *Canon,* pp. 288–97.)

[14]Eusebius, *Ecclesiastical History* 6.15.2. Origen died about A.D. 254. Origen names all the books of the present Old Testament canon except the twelve minor prophets

to be read by those who newly join us, and who wish for instruction in the word of godliness."[15] However, other early church leaders did quote several of these books as Scripture.[16]

There are doctrinal and historical inconsistencies with a number of these books. E. J. Young notes:

> There are no marks in these books which would attest a divine origin. . . . both Judith and Tobit contain historical, chronological and geographical errors. The books justify falsehood and deception and make salvation to depend upon works of merit. . . . Ecclesiasticus and the Wisdom of Solomon inculcate a morality based upon expediency. Wisdom teaches the creation of the world out of pre-existent matter (11:17). Ecclesiasticus teaches that the giving of alms makes atonement for sin (3:30). In Baruch it is said that God hears the prayers of the dead (3:4), and in I Maccabees there are historical and geographical errors.[17]

It was not until 1546, at the Council of Trent, that the Roman Catholic Church officially declared the Apocrypha to be part of the canon (with the exception of 1 and 2 Esdras and the Prayer of Manasseh). It is significant that the Council of Trent was the response of the Roman Catholic Church to the teachings of Martin Luther and the rapidly spreading Protestant Reformation, and the books of the Apocrypha contain support for the Catholic teaching of prayers for the dead and justification by faith plus works, not by faith alone. In affirming the Apocrypha as within the canon, Roman Catholics would hold that the church has the authority to constitute a literary work as "Scripture," while Protestants have held that the church cannot make something to be Scripture, but can only recognize what God has already caused to be written as his own words.[18] (One analogy here would be to say that a police investigator can recognize counterfeit money as counterfeit and can recognize genuine money as genuine, but he cannot make counterfeit money to be genuine, nor can any declaration by any number of police make counterfeit money to be something it is not. Only the official treasury of a nation can make money that is real money; similarly, only God can make words to be his very words and worthy of inclusion in Scripture.)

Thus the writings of the Apocrypha should not be regarded as part of Scripture: (1) they do not claim for themselves the same kind of authority as the Old Testament writings; (2) they were not regarded as God's words by the Jewish people from whom they

---

(which would be counted as one book), but this leaves his list of "twenty-two books" incomplete at twenty-one, so apparently Eusebius's citation is incomplete, at least in the form we have it today.

Eusebius himself elsewhere repeats the statement of the Jewish historian Josephus that the Scriptures contain twenty-two books, but nothing since the time of Artaxerxes (3.10.1 – 5), and this would exclude all of the Apocrypha.

[15]Athanasius, *Letter 39*, in *Nicene and Post Nicene Fathers*, 2d ser., ed. Philip Schaff and Henry Wace (Grand Rapids: Eerdmans, 1978), vol. 4: *Athanasius*, pp. 551 – 52.

[16]See Metzger, *Apocrypha*, pp. xii – xiii. Metzger notes that

none of the early Latin and Greek church fathers who quoted from the Apocrypha as Scripture knew any Hebrew. Beckwith, *Canon*, pp. 386 – 89, argues that the evidence of Christian writers quoting the Apocrypha as Scripture is considerably less extensive and less significant than scholars often claim it to be.

[17]E. J. Young, "The Canon of the Old Testament," in *Revelation and the Bible*, pp. 167 – 68.

[18]It should be noted that Roman Catholics use the term *deuterocanonical* rather than *apocryphal* to refer to these books. They understand this to mean "later added to the canon" (the prefix *deutero-* means "second").

originated; (3) they were not considered to be Scripture by Jesus or the New Testament authors; and (4) they contain teachings inconsistent with the rest of the Bible. We must conclude that they are merely human words, not God-breathed words like the words of Scripture. They do have value for historical and linguistic research, and they contain a number of helpful stories about the courage and faith of many Jews during the period after the Old Testament ends, but they have never been part of the Old Testament canon, and they should not be thought of as part of the Bible. Therefore, they have no binding authority for the thought or life of Christians today.

In conclusion, with regard to the canon of the Old Testament, Christians today should have no worry that anything needed has been left out or that anything that is not God's words has been included.

## B. The New Testament Canon

The development of the New Testament canon begins with the writings of the apostles. It should be remembered that the writing of Scripture primarily occurs in connection with God's great acts in redemptive history. The Old Testament records and interprets for us the calling of Abraham and the lives of his descendants, the exodus from Egypt and the wilderness wanderings, the establishment of God's people in the land of Canaan, the establishment of the monarchy, and the Exile and return from captivity. Each of these great acts of God in history is interpreted for us in God's own words in Scripture. The Old Testament closes with the expectation of the Messiah to come (Mal. 3:1–4; 4:1–6). The next stage in redemptive history is the coming of the Messiah, and it is not surprising that no further Scripture would be written until this next and greatest event in the history of redemption occurred.

This is why the New Testament consists of the writings of the apostles.[19] It is primarily the apostles who are given the ability from the Holy Spirit to recall accurately the words and deeds of Jesus and to interpret them rightly for subsequent generations.

Jesus promised this empowering to his disciples (who were called apostles after the resurrection) in John 14:26: "But the Counselor, the Holy Spirit, whom the Father will send in my name, he will teach you all things, and bring to your remembrance all that I have said to you." Similarly, Jesus promised further revelation of truth from the Holy Spirit when he told his disciples, "When the Spirit of truth comes, he will guide you into all the truth; for he will not speak on his own authority, but whatever he hears he will speak, and he will declare to you the things that are to come. He will glorify me, for he will take what is mine and declare it to you" (John 16:13–14). In these verses the disciples are promised amazing gifts to enable them to write Scripture: the Holy Spirit would teach them "all things," would cause them to remember "all" that Jesus had said, and would guide them into "all the truth "

Furthermore, those who have the office of apostle in the early church are seen to claim an authority equal to that of the Old Testament prophets, an authority to speak and write

---

[19]A few New Testament books (Mark, Luke, Acts, Hebrews, and Jude) were not written by apostles but by others closely associated with them and apparently authorized by them: see the discussion below, pp. 48–49.

words that are God's very words. Peter encourages his readers to remember "the commandment of the Lord and Savior through your apostles" (2 Peter 3:2). To lie to the apostles (Acts 5:2) is equivalent to lying to the Holy Spirit (Acts 5:3) and lying to God (Acts 5:4).

This claim to be able to speak words that were the words of God himself is especially frequent in the writings of the apostle Paul. He claims not only that the Holy Spirit has revealed to him "what no eye has seen, nor ear heard, nor the heart of man conceived" (1 Cor. 2:9), but also that when he declares this revelation, he speaks it "in words not taught by human wisdom but taught by the Spirit, interpreting Spiritual things in Spiritual words" (1 Cor. 2:13, author's translation).[20]

Similarly, Paul tells the Corinthians, "If any one thinks that he is a prophet, or spiritual, he should acknowledge that what I am writing to you is a command of the Lord" (1 Cor. 14:37). The word translated "what" in this verse is a plural relative pronoun in Greek (*ha*) and more literally could be translated "*the things* that I am writing to you." Thus, Paul claims that his directives to the church at Corinth are not merely his own but a command of the Lord. Later, in defending his apostolic office, Paul says that he will give the Corinthians "proof that Christ is speaking in me" (2 Cor. 13:3). Other similar verses could be mentioned (for example, Rom. 2:16; Gal. 1:8–9; 1 Thess. 2:13; 4:8, 15; 5:27; 2 Thess. 3:6, 14).

The apostles, then, have authority to write words that are God's own words, equal in truth status and authority to the words of the Old Testament Scriptures. They do this to record, interpret, and apply to the lives of believers the great truths about the life, death, and resurrection of Christ.

It would not be surprising therefore to find some of the New Testament writings being placed with the Old Testament Scriptures as part of the canon of Scripture. In fact, this is what we find in at least two instances. In 2 Peter 3:16, Peter shows not only an awareness of the existence of written epistles from Paul, but also a clear willingness to classify "all of his [Paul's] epistles" with "the other scriptures": Peter says, "So also our beloved brother Paul wrote to you according to the wisdom given him, speaking of this as he does in all his letters. There are some things in them hard to understand, which the ignorant and unstable twist to their own destruction, *as they do the other scriptures*" (2 Peter 3:15–16). The word translated "scriptures" here is *graphē*, a word that occurs fifty-one times in the New Testament and that refers to the Old Testament Scriptures in every one of those occurrences. Thus, the word *Scripture* was a technical term for the New Testament authors, and it was used only of those writings that were thought to be God's words and therefore part of the canon of Scripture. But in this verse, Peter classifies Paul's writings with the "other Scriptures" (meaning the Old Testament Scriptures). Paul's writings are therefore considered by Peter also to be worthy of the title "Scripture" and thus worthy of inclusion in the canon.

A second instance is found in 1 Timothy 5:17–18. Paul says, "Let the elders who rule well be considered worthy of double honor, especially those who labor in preaching and

---

[20]This is my own translation of the last phrase of 1 Cor. 2:13: see Wayne Grudem, "Scripture's Self-Attestation," in *Scripture and Truth*, ed. D. A. Carson and John Woodbridge (Grand Rapids: Zondervan, 1983), p. 365, n. 61. But this translation is not crucial to the main point: namely, that Paul speaks words taught by the Holy Spirit, a point that is affirmed in the first part of the verse, no matter how the second half is translated.

teaching; *for the scripture* says, 'You shall not muzzle an ox when it is treading out the grain,' and, 'The laborer deserves his wages.'" The first quotation from "Scripture" is found in Deuteronomy 25:4, but the second quotation, "The laborer deserves his wages," is found nowhere in the Old Testament. It does occur, however, in Luke 10:7 (with exactly the same words in the Greek text). So here we have Paul apparently quoting a portion of Luke's gospel[21] and calling it "Scripture," that is, something that is to be considered part of the canon.[22] In both of these passages (2 Peter 3:16 and 1 Tim. 5.17–18) we see evidence that very early in the history of the church the writings of the New Testament began to be accepted as part of the canon.

Because the apostles, by virtue of their apostolic office, had authority to write words of Scripture, the authentic written teachings of the apostles were accepted by the early church as part of the canon of Scripture. If we accept the arguments for the traditional views of authorship of the New Testament writings,[23] then we have most of the New Testament in the canon because of direct authorship by the apostles. This would include Matthew; John; Romans to Philemon (all of the Pauline epistles); James;[24] 1 and 2 Peter; 1, 2, and 3 John; and Revelation.

This leaves five books, Mark, Luke, Acts, Hebrews, and Jude, which were not written by apostles. The details of the historical process by which these books came to be counted as part of Scripture by the early church are scarce, but Mark, Luke, and Acts were commonly acknowledged very early, probably because of the close association of Mark with the apostle Peter, and of Luke (the author of Luke-Acts) with the apostle Paul. Similarly, Jude apparently was accepted by virtue of the author's connection with James (see Jude 1) and the fact that he was the brother of Jesus.[25]

The acceptance of Hebrews as canonical was urged by many in the church on the basis of an assumed Pauline authorship. But from very early times there were others who rejected Pauline authorship in favor of one or another of several different suggestions. Origen, who died about A.D. 254, mentions various theories of authorship and concludes, "But who actually wrote the epistle, only God knows."[26] Thus, the acceptance of Hebrews as canonical was not entirely due to a belief in Pauline authorship. Rather, the intrinsic qualities of the book itself must have finally convinced early readers, as they continue to convince believers today, that whoever its human author may have been, its ultimate author can only have been God himself. The majestic glory of Christ shines forth from the pages of the epistle to the Hebrews so brightly

---

[21]Someone might object that Paul could be quoting an oral tradition of Jesus' words rather than Luke's gospel, but it is doubtful that Paul would call any oral tradition "Scripture," since the word (Gk. *graphē*, "writing") is always in New Testament usage applied to written texts, and since Paul's close association with Luke makes it very possible that he would quote Luke's written gospel.

[22]Luke himself was not an apostle, but his gospel is here accorded authority equal with that of the apostolic writings. Apparently this was due to his very close association with the apostles, especially Paul, and the endorsement of his gospel by an apostle.

[23]For a defense of traditional views of authorship of the New Testament writings, see Donald Guthrie, *New Testament Introduction* (Downers Grove, Ill.: InterVarsity Press, 1970).

[24]James seems to be considered an apostle in 1 Cor. 15:7 and Gal. 1:19. He also fulfills functions appropriate to an apostle in Acts 12:17; 15:13; 21:18; Gal. 2:9, 12.

[25]The acceptance of Jude in the canon was slow, primarily because of doubts concerning his quotation of the noncanonical book of 1 Enoch.

[26]Origen's statement is quoted in Eusebius, *Ecclesiastical History,* 6.25.14.

that no believer who reads it seriously should ever want to question its place in the canon.

This brings us to the heart of the question of canonicity. For a book to belong in the canon, it is absolutely necessary that the book have divine authorship. If the words of the book are God's words (through human authors), and if the early church, under the direction of the apostles, preserved the book as part of Scripture, then the book belongs in the canon. But if the words of the book are not God's words, it does not belong in the canon. The question of authorship by an apostle is important because it was primarily the apostles to whom Christ gave the ability to write words with absolute divine authority. If a writing can be shown to be by an apostle, then its absolute divine authority is automatically established.[27] Thus, the early church automatically accepted as part of the canon the written teachings of the apostles which the apostles wanted preserved as Scripture.

But the existence of some New Testament writings that were not authored directly by apostles shows that there were others in the early church to whom Christ also gave the ability, through the work of the Holy Spirit, to write words that were God's own words and also therefore intended to be part of the canon. In these cases, the early church had the task of recognizing which writings had the characteristic of being God's own words (through human authors).

For some books (at least Mark, Luke, and Acts, and perhaps Hebrews and Jude as well), the church had, at least in some areas, the personal testimony of some living apostles to affirm the absolute divine authority of these books. For example, Paul would have affirmed the authenticity of Luke and Acts, and Peter would have affirmed the authenticity of Mark as containing the gospel which he himself preached. In other cases, and in some geographical areas, the church simply had to decide whether it heard the voice of God himself speaking in the words of these writings. In these cases, the words of these books would have been *self-attesting;* that is, the words would have borne witness to their own divine authorship as Christians read them. This seems to have been the case with Hebrews.

It should not surprise us that the early church should have been able to recognize Hebrews and other writings, not written by apostles, as God's very words. Had not Jesus said "My sheep hear my voice" (John 10:27)? It should not be thought impossible or unlikely, therefore, that the early church would be able to use a combination of factors, including apostolic endorsement, consistency with the rest of Scripture, and the perception of a writing as "God-breathed" on the part of an overwhelming majority of

---

[27]Of course, this does not mean that everything an apostle wrote, including even grocery lists and receipts for business transactions, would be considered Scripture. We are speaking here of writings done when acting in the role of an apostle and giving apostolic instructions to churches and to individual Christians (such as Timothy or Philemon).

It is also very likely that the living apostles themselves gave some guidance to the churches concerning which works they intended to be preserved and used as Scripture in the churches (see Col. 4:16; 2 Thess. 3:14; 2 Peter 3:16).

There were apparently some writings that had absolute divine authority but that the apostles did not decide to preserve as "Scripture" for the churches (such as Paul's "previous letter" to the Corinthians: see 1 Cor. 5:9). Moreover, the apostles did much more oral teaching, which had divine authority (see 2 Thess. 2:15) but was not written down and preserved as Scripture. Thus, in addition to apostolic authorship, preservation by the church under the direction of the apostles was necessary for a work to be included in the canon.

believers, to decide that a writing was in fact God's words (through a human author) and therefore worthy of inclusion in the canon. Nor should it be thought unlikely that the church would be able to use this process over a period of time—as writings were circulated to various parts of the early church—and finally to come to a completely correct decision, without excluding any writings that were in fact "God-breathed" and without including any that were not.[28]

In A.D. 367 the Thirty-ninth Paschal Letter of Athanasius contained an exact list of the twenty-seven New Testament books we have today. This was the list of books accepted by the churches in the eastern part of the Mediterranean world. Thirty years later, in A.D. 397, the Council of Carthage, representing the churches in the western part of the Mediterranean world, agreed with the eastern churches on the same list. These are the earliest final lists of our present-day canon.

Should we expect any more writings to be added to the canon? The opening sentence in Hebrews puts this question in the proper historical perspective, the perspective of the history of redemption: "In many and various ways God spoke of old to our fathers by the prophets; but in these last days he has spoken to us by a Son, whom he appointed the heir of all things, through whom also he created the world" (Heb. 1:1–2).

The contrast between the former speaking "of old" by the prophets and the recent speaking "in these last days" suggests that God's speech to us by his Son is the culmination of his speaking to mankind and is his greatest and final revelation to mankind in this period of redemptive history. The exceptional greatness of the revelation that comes through the Son, far exceeding any revelation in the old covenant, is emphasized again and again throughout chapters 1 and 2 of Hebrews. These facts all indicate that there is a finality to the revelation of God in Christ and that once this revelation has been completed, no more is to be expected.

But where do we learn about this revelation through Christ? The New Testament writings contain the final, authoritative, and sufficient interpretation of Christ's work of redemption. The apostles and their close companions report Christ's words and deeds and interpret them with absolute divine authority. When they have finished their writing, there is no more to be added with the same absolute divine authority. Thus, once the writings of the New Testament apostles and their authorized companions are completed, we have in written form the final record of everything that God wants us to know about the life, death, and resurrection of Christ, and its meaning for the lives of believers for all time. Since this is God's greatest revelation for mankind, no more is to be expected once this is complete. In this way, then, Hebrews 1:1–2 shows us why no more writings can be added to the Bible after the time of the New Testament. The canon is now closed.

A similar kind of consideration may be drawn from Revelation 22:18–19:

> I warn every one who hears the words of the prophecy of this book: if any one adds to them, God will add to him the plagues described in this book, and if any one takes away from the words of the book of this prophecy, God will take

---

[28]I am not discussing here the question of textual variants (that is, differences in individual words and phrases found among the many ancient copies of Scripture that still exist). This question is treated in chapter 5, sections 3 and 4.

away his share in the tree of life and in the holy city, which are described in this book.

The primary reference of these verses is clearly to the book of Revelation itself, for John refers to his writing as "the words of the prophecy of this book" in verses 7 and 10 of this chapter (and the entire book is called a prophecy in Rev. 1:3). Furthermore, the reference to "the tree of life and . . . the holy city, which are described in this book" indicates that the book of Revelation itself is intended.

It is, however, not accidental that this statement comes at the end of the last chapter of Revelation, and that Revelation is the last book in the New Testament. In fact, Revelation has to be placed last in the canon. For many books, their placement in the assembling of the canon is of little consequence. But just as Genesis must be placed first (for it tells us of creation), so Revelation must be placed last (for its focus is to tell us of the future and God's new creation). The events described in Revelation are historically subsequent to the events described in the rest of the New Testament and require that Revelation be placed where it is. Thus, it is not inappropriate for us to understand this exceptionally strong warning at the end of Revelation as applying in a secondary way to the whole of Scripture. Placed here, where it must be placed, the warning forms an appropriate conclusion to the entire canon of Scripture. Along with Hebrews 1:1–2 and the history-of-redemption perspective implicit in those verses, this broader application of Revelation 22:18–19 also suggests to us that we should expect no more Scripture to be added beyond what we already have.

How do we know, then, that we have the right books in the canon of Scripture we now possess? The question can be answered in two different ways. First, if we are asking upon what we should base our confidence, the answer must ultimately be that our confidence is based on the faithfulness of God. We know that God loves his people, and it is supremely important that God's people have his own words, for they are our life (Deut. 32:47; Matt. 4:4). They are more precious, more important to us than anything else in this world. We also know that God our Father is in control of all history, and he is not the kind of Father who will trick us or fail to be faithful to us or keep from us something we absolutely need.

The severity of the punishments in Revelation 22:18–19 that come to those who add to or take from God's words also confirms the importance for God's people of having a correct canon. There could be no greater punishments than these, for they are the punishments of eternal judgment. This shows that God himself places supreme value on our having a correct collection of God-breathed writings, no more and no less. In the light of this fact, could it be right for us to believe that God our Father, who controls all history, would allow all of his church for almost two thousand years to be deprived of something he himself values so highly and is so necessary for our spiritual lives?[29]

---

[29]This is of course not to affirm the impossible notion that God providentially preserves every word in every copy of every text, no matter how careless the copyist, or that he must miraculously provide every believer with a Bible instantly. Nevertheless, this consideration of God's faithful care of his children should certainly cause us to be thankful that in God's providence there is no significantly attested textual variant that would change any point of Christian doctrine or ethics, so faithfully has the text been transmitted and preserved. However, we must say clearly that there are a number of differing words in the different ancient manuscripts of the Bible that are preserved today. These are called "textual variants." The question of textual variants within the surviving manuscripts of the books that belong in the canon is discussed in chapter 5, p. 80–81.

The preservation and correct assembling of the canon of Scripture should ultimately be seen by believers, then, not as part of church history subsequent to God's great central acts of redemption for his people, but as an integral part of the history of redemption itself. Just as God was at work in creation, in the calling of his people Israel, in the life, death, and resurrection of Christ, and in the early work and writings of the apostles, so God was at work in the preservation and assembling together of the books of Scripture for the benefit of his people for the entire church age. Ultimately, then, we base our confidence in the correctness of our present canon on the faithfulness of God.

The question of how we know that we have the right books can, secondly, be answered in a somewhat different way. We might wish to focus on the process by which we become persuaded that the books we have now in the canon are the right ones. In this process two factors are at work: the activity of the Holy Spirit convincing us as we read Scripture for ourselves, and the historical data that we have available for our consideration.

As we read Scripture the Holy Spirit works to convince us that the books we have in Scripture are all from God and are his words to us. It has been the testimony of Christians throughout the ages that as they read the books of the Bible, the words of Scripture speak to their hearts as no other books do. Day after day, year after year, Christians find that the words of the Bible are indeed the words of God speaking to them with an authority, a power, and a persuasiveness that no other writings possess. Truly the Word of God is "living and active, sharper than any two-edged sword, piercing to the division of soul and spirit, of joints and marrow, and discerning the thoughts and intentions of the heart" (Heb. 4:12).

Yet the process by which we become persuaded that the present canon is right is also helped by historical data. Of course, if the assembling of the canon was one part of God's central acts in the history of redemption (as was stated above), then Christians today should not presume to take it upon themselves to attempt to add to or subtract from the books of the canon: the process was completed long ago. Nevertheless, a thorough investigation of the historical circumstances surrounding the assembling of the canon is helpful in confirming our conviction that the decisions made by the early church were correct decisions. Some of this historical data has been mentioned in the preceding pages. Other, more detailed data is available for those who wish to pursue more specialized investigations.[30]

Yet one further historical fact should be mentioned. Today there exist no strong candidates for addition to the canon and no strong objections to any book presently in the canon. Of those writings that some in the early church wanted to include in the canon, it is safe to say that there are none that present-day evangelicals would want to include.

[30]A very helpful recent survey of this field is David Dunbar, "The Biblical Canon," in *Hermeneutics, Authority, and Canon,* ed. D. A. Carson and John Woodbridge (Grand Rapids: Zondervan, 1986), pp. 295–360. In addition, three recent books are of such excellent quality that they will define the discussion of canon for many years to come: Roger Beckwith, *The Old Testament Canon of the New Testament Church and Its Background in Early Judaism* (London: SPCK, 1985, and Grand Rapids: Eerdmans, 1986); Bruce Metzger, *The Canon of the New Testament: Its Origin, Development, and Significance* (Oxford: Clarendon; New York: Oxford University Press, 1987); and F. F. Bruce, *The Canon of Scripture* (Downers Grove, Ill.: InterVarsity Press, 1988).

Some of the very early writers distinguished themselves quite clearly from the apostles and their writings from the writings of the apostles. Ignatius, for example, about A.D. 110, said, "I do not order you as did Peter and Paul; *they were apostles,* I am a convict; they were free, I am even until now a slave" (Ignatius, *To the Romans,* 4.3; compare the attitude toward the apostles in 1 Clement 42:1, 2; 44:1–2 [A.D. 95]; Ignatius, *To the Magnesians,* 7:1; 13:1–2, et al.).

Even those writings that were for a time thought by some to be worthy of inclusion in the canon contain doctrinal teaching that is contradictory to the rest of Scripture. "The Shepherd" of Hermas, for example, teaches "the necessity of penance" and "the possibility of the forgiveness of sins at least once after baptism. . . . The author seems to identify the Holy Spirit with the Son of God before the Incarnation, and to hold that the Trinity came into existence only after the humanity of Christ had been taken up into heaven" (*Oxford Dictionary of the Christian Church,* p. 641).

The *Gospel of Thomas,* which for a time was held by some to belong to the canon, ends with the following absurd statement (par. 114):

> Simon Peter said to them: "Let Mary go away from us, for women are not worthy of life." Jesus said: "Lo, I shall lead her, so that I may make her a male, that she too may become a living spirit, resembling you males. For every woman who makes herself a male will enter the kingdom of heaven."[31]

All other existing documents that had in the early church any possibility of inclusion in the canon are similar to these in that they either contain explicit disclaimers of canonical status or include some doctrinal aberrations that clearly make them unworthy of inclusion in the Bible.[32]

On the other hand, there are no strong objections to any book currently in the canon. In the case of several New Testament books that were slow to gain approval by the whole church (books such as 2 Peter or 2 and 3 John), much of the early hesitancy over their inclusion can be attributed to the fact that they were not initially circulated very widely, and that full knowledge of the contents of all the New Testament writings spread through the church rather slowly. (Martin Luther's hesitancies concerning James are quite understandable in view of the doctrinal controversy in which he was engaged, but such hesitancy

---

[31]This document was not written by Thomas the apostle. Current scholarly opinion attributes it to an unknown author in the second century A.D. who used Thomas's name.

[32]It is appropriate here to say a word about the writing called the *Didache.* Although this document was not considered for inclusion in the canon during the early history of the church, many scholars have thought it to be a very early document and some today quote it as if it were an authority on the teaching of the early church on the same level as the New Testament writings. It was first discovered in 1875 at a library in Constantinople but probably dates from the first or second century A.D. Yet it contradicts or adds to the commands of the New Testament at many points. For example, Christians are told to let alms sweat in their hands until they know to whom they are giving (1.6); food offered to idols is forbidden (6.3); people are required to fast before baptism, and baptism must be done in running water (7.1–4); fasting is required on Wednesdays and Fridays but prohibited on Mondays and Thursdays (8.1); Christians are required to pray the Lord's Prayer three times a day (8.3); unbaptized persons are excluded from the Lord's Supper, and prayers unknown in the New Testament are given as a pattern for celebrating the Lord's Supper (9.1–5); apostles are prohibited from staying in a city more than two days (11.5; but note that Paul stayed a year and a half in Corinth and three years in Ephesus!); prophets who speak in the Spirit cannot be tested or examined (11.7, in contradiction to 1 Cor. 14:29 and 1 Thess. 5:20–21); salvation requires perfection at the last time (16.2). Such a document, of unknown authorship, is hardly a reliable guide for the teachings and practices of the early church.

was certainly not necessary. The apparent doctrinal conflict with Paul's teaching is easily resolved once it is recognized that James is using three key terms, *justification, faith,* and *works* in senses different from those with which Paul used them.)[33]

There is therefore historical confirmation for the correctness of the current canon. Yet it must be remembered in connection with any historical investigation that the work of the early church was not to bestow divine authority or even ecclesiastical authority upon some merely human writings, but rather to recognize the divinely authored characteristic of writings that already had such a quality. This is because the ultimate criterion of canonicity is divine authorship, not human or ecclesiastical approval.

At this point someone may ask a hypothetical question about what we should do if another one of Paul's epistles were discovered, for example. Would we add it to Scripture? This is a difficult question, because two conflicting considerations are involved. On the one hand, if a great majority of believers were convinced that this was indeed an authentic Pauline epistle, written in the course of Paul's fulfillment of his apostolic office, then the nature of Paul's apostolic authority would guarantee that the writing would be God's very words (as well as Paul's), and that its teachings would be consistent with the rest of Scripture. But the fact that it was not preserved as part of the canon would indicate that it was not among the writings the apostles wanted the church to preserve as part of Scripture. Moreover, it must immediately be said that such a hypothetical question is just that: hypothetical. It is exceptionally difficult to imagine what kind of historical data might be discovered that could convincingly demonstrate to the church as a whole that a letter lost for over 1,900 years was genuinely authored by Paul, and it is more difficult still to understand how our sovereign God could have faithfully cared for his people for over 1,900 years and still allowed them to be continually deprived of something he intended them to have as part of his final revelation of himself in Jesus Christ. These considerations make it so highly improbable that any such manuscript would be discovered at some time in the future, that such a hypothetical question really does not merit further serious consideration.

In conclusion, are there any books in our present canon that should not be there? No. We can rest our confidence in this fact in the faithfulness of God our Father, who would not lead all his people for nearly two thousand years to trust as his Word something that is not. And we find our confidence repeatedly confirmed both by historical investigation and by the work of the Holy Spirit in enabling us to hear God's voice in a unique way as we read from every one of the sixty-six books in our present canon of Scripture.

But are there any missing books, books that should have been included in Scripture but were not? The answer must be no. In all known literature there are no candidates that even come close to Scripture when consideration is given both to their doctrinal consistency with the rest of Scripture and to the type of authority they claim for themselves (as well as the way those claims of authority have been received by other believers). Once again, God's faithfulness to his people convinces us that there is nothing missing

---

[33]See R. V. G. Tasker, *The General Epistle of James,* TNTC (London: Tyndale Press, 1956), pp. 67–71. Although Luther placed James near the end of his German translation of the New Testament, he did not exclude it from the canon, and he cited over half of the verses in James as authoritative in various parts of his writings (see Douglas Moo, *The Letter of James,* TNTC [Leicester and Downers Grove, Ill.: InterVarsity Press, 1985], p. 18; see also pp. 100–117 on faith and works in James).

from Scripture that God thinks we need to know for obeying him and trusting him fully. The canon of Scripture today is exactly what God wanted it to be, and it will stay that way until Christ returns.

## QUESTIONS FOR PERSONAL APPLICATION

1. Why is it important to your Christian life to know which writings are God's words and which are not? How would your relationship with God be different if you had to look for his words that were scattered among all the writings of Christians throughout church history? How would your Christian life be different if God's words were contained not only in the Bible but also in the official declarations of the church throughout history?

2. Have you had doubts or questions about the canonicity of any of the books of the Bible? What caused those questions? What should one do to resolve them?

3. Mormons, Jehovah's Witnesses, and members of other cults have claimed present-day revelations from God that they count equal to the Bible in authority. What reasons can you give to indicate the falsity of those claims? In practice, do these people treat the Bible as an authority equal to these other "revelations"?

4. If you have never read any parts of the Old Testament Apocrypha, perhaps you would want to read some sections.[34] Do you feel you can trust these writings in the same way you trust Scripture? Compare the effect these writings have on you with the effect Scripture has on you. You might want to make a similar comparison with some writings from a collection of books called the New Testament Apocrypha,[35] or perhaps with the *Book of Mormon* or the *Qur'an*. Is the spiritual effect of these writings on your life positive or negative? How does it compare with the spiritual effect the Bible has on your life?

## SPECIAL TERMS

| | |
|---|---|
| Apocrypha | covenant |
| apostle | God-breathed |
| canon | history of redemption |
| canonical | self-attesting |

---

[34]A good recent translation is *The Oxford Annotated Apocrypha* (*RSV*), ed. Bruce M. Metzger (New York: Oxford University Press, 1965). There is also a collection of nonbiblical writings from the time of the New Testament called "New Testament apocrypha" (see next note), but these are much less commonly read. When people speak of "the Apocrypha" without further specification, they are referring only to the Old Testament Apocrypha.

[35]E. Hennecke, *New Testament Apocrypha,* ed. W. Schneemelcher; English trans. ed. R. McL. Wilson (2 vols.: SCM Press, 1965). It should also be noted that some other, more orthodox literature from the early church can be found conveniently in a collection of writings referred to as the "Apostolic Fathers." A good translation is found in Kirsopp Lake, trans., *The Apostolic Fathers,* Loeb Classical Library (2 vols.: Cambridge, Mass.: Harvard University Press, 1912, 1913), but other useful translations are also available.

## BIBLIOGRAPHY

Beckwith, R. T. "Canon of the Old Testament." In *IBD,* 1:235–38.

Beckwith, Roger. *The Old Testament Canon of the New Testament Church and Its Background in Early Judaism.* Grand Rapids: Eerdmans, 1985.

Birdsall, J. N. "Apocrypha." In *IBD,* 1:75–77.

_____. "Canon of the New Testament." In *IBD,* 1:240–45.

Bruce, F. F. *The Canon of Scripture.* Downers Grove, Ill: InterVarsity Press, 1988.

Carson, D. A., and John D. Woodbridge, eds. *Hermeneutics, Authority, and Canon.* Grand Rapids: Zondervan, 1986.

Dunbar, David G. "The Biblical Canon." In *Hermeneutics, Authority, and Canon.* Ed. by D. A. Carson and John Woodbridge. Grand Rapids: Zondervan, 1986.

Green, William Henry. *General Introduction to the Old Testament: The Canon.* New York: Scribners, 1898.

Harris, R. Laird. "Chronicles and the Canon in New Testament Times." *JETS.* Vol. 33, no. 1 (March 1990): 75–84.

_____. *Inspiration and Canonicity of the Bible: An Historical and Exegetical Study.* Grand Rapids: Zondervan, 1989.

Kline, Meredith G. *The Structure of Biblical Authority.* Grand Rapids: Eerdmans, 1972.

Leiman, S. Z. *The Canonization of Hebrew Scripture: The Talmudic and Midrashic Evidence.* Hamden, Conn.: Archon, 1976.

McRay, J. R. "Bible, Canon of." In *EDT,* pp. 140–41.

Metzger, Bruce M. *The Canon of the New Testament: Its Origin, Development, and Significance.* Oxford: Clarendon; and New York: Oxford University Press, 1987.

Packer, J. I. "Scripture." *NDT,* 627–31.

Ridderbos, Herman N. *Redemptive History and the New Testament Scriptures.* Formerly, *The Authority of the New Testament Scriptures.* 2d rev. ed. Trans. by H. D. Jongste. Rev. by Richard B. Gaffin, Jr. Phillipsburg, N.J.: Presbyterian and Reformed, 1988.

Westcott, Brooke Foss. *The Bible in the Church: A Popular Account of the Collection and Reception of the Holy Scriptures in the Christian Churches.* First ed. with alterations. London: Macmillan, 1901.

Zahn, Theodor. *Geschichte des Neutestamentlichen Kanons.* 2 vols. Erlangen: Deichert, 1888–90. Reprint ed., Hildesheim and New York: Olms, 1975.

## SCRIPTURE MEMORY PASSAGE

**Hebrews 1:1–2:** *In many and various ways God spoke of old to our fathers by the prophets; but in these last days he has spoken to us by a Son, whom he appointed the heir of all things, through whom also he created the world.*

# HYMN

## "O Word of God Incarnate"

O Word of God incarnate, O wisdom from on high,
O truth unchanged, unchanging, O light of our dark sky;
We praise thee for the radiance that from the hallowed page,
A lantern to our footsteps, shines on from age to age.

The church from her dear Master received the gift divine,
And still that light she lifteth o'er all the earth to shine.
It is the golden casket, where gems of truth are stored;
It is the heav'n-drawn picture of Christ, the Living Word.

It floateth like a banner before God's host unfurled;
It shineth like a beacon above the darkling world.
It is the chart and compass that o'er life's surging sea,
'Mid mists and rocks and quicksands, still guides, O Christ, to thee.

O make thy church, dear Savior, a lamp of purest gold,
To bear before the nations thy true light, as of old.
O teach thy wand'ring pilgrims by this their path to trace,
Till, clouds and darkness ended, they see thee face to face.

AUTHOR: WILLIAM WALSHAM HOW, 1867

# Chapter 4

# THE FOUR CHARACTERISTICS OF SCRIPTURE: (1) AUTHORITY

## *How do we know that the Bible is God's Word?*

In the previous chapter our goal was to determine which writings belong in the Bible and which writings do not. But once we have determined what the Bible is, our next step is to ask what it is like. What does the whole Bible teach us about itself?

The major teachings of the Bible about itself can be classified into four characteristics (sometimes termed attributes): (1) the authority of Scripture; (2) the clarity of Scripture; (3) the necessity of Scripture; and (4) the sufficiency of Scripture.

With regard to the first characteristic, most Christians would agree that the Bible is our authority in some sense. But in exactly what sense does the Bible claim to be our authority? And how do we become persuaded that the claims of Scripture to be God's Word are true? These are the questions addressed in this chapter.

## EXPLANATION AND SCRIPTURAL BASIS

*The authority of Scripture means that all the words in Scripture are God's words in such a way that to disbelieve or disobey any word of Scripture is to disbelieve or disobey God.*

This definition may now be examined in its various parts.

### A. All the Words in Scripture Are God's Words

**1. This Is What the Bible Claims for Itself.** There are frequent claims in the Bible that all the words of Scripture are God's words (as well as words that were written down by men).[1] In the Old Testament, this is frequently seen in the introductory phrase,

---

[1] Of course, I do not mean to say that every word in Scripture was audibly spoken by God himself, since the Bible records the words of hundreds of different people, such as King David and Peter and even Satan himself. But I do mean that even the quotations of other people are *God's* reports of what they said, and, rightly interpreted in their contexts, come to us with God's authority.

"Thus says the LORD," which appears hundreds of times. In the world of the Old Testament, this phrase would have been recognized as identical in form to the phrase, "Thus says king . . . ," which was used to preface the edict of a king to his subjects, an edict that could not be challenged or questioned but that simply had to be obeyed.[2] Thus, when the prophets say, "Thus says the Lord," they are claiming to be messengers from the sovereign King of Israel, namely, God himself, and they are claiming that their words are the absolutely authoritative words of God. When a prophet spoke in God's name in this way, every word he spoke had to come from God, or he would be a false prophet (cf. Num. 22:38; Deut. 18:18–20; Jer. 1:9; 14:14; 23:16–22; 29:31–32; Ezek. 2:7; 13:1–16).

Furthermore, God is often said to speak "through" the prophet (1 Kings 14:18; 16:12, 34; 2 Kings 9:36; 14:25; Jer. 37:2; Zech. 7:7, 12). Thus, what the prophet says in God's name, God says (1 Kings 13:26 with v. 21; 1 Kings 21:19 with 2 Kings 9:25–26; Hag. 1:12; cf. 1 Sam. 15:3, 18). In these and other instances in the Old Testament, words that the prophets spoke can equally be referred to as words that God himself spoke. Thus, to disbelieve or disobey anything a prophet says is to disbelieve or disobey God himself (Deut. 18:19; 1 Sam. 10:8; 13:13–14; 15:3, 19, 23; 1 Kings 20:35, 36).

These verses of course do not claim that *all* the words in the Old Testament are God's words, for these verses themselves are referring only to specific sections of spoken or written words in the Old Testament. But the cumulative force of these passages, including the hundreds of passages that begin "Thus says the Lord," is to demonstrate that within the Old Testament we have written records of words that are said to be God's own words. These words when written down constitute large sections of the Old Testament.

In the New Testament, a number of passages indicate that all of the Old Testament writings are thought of as God's words. Second Timothy 3:16 says, "All Scripture is God-breathed and is useful for teaching, rebuking, correcting and training in righteousness" (NIV).[3] Here "Scripture" (*graphē*) must refer to the Old Testament written Scripture, for that is what the word *graphē* refers to in every one of its fifty-one occurrences in the New Testament.[4] Furthermore, the "sacred writings" of the Old Testament are what Paul[5] has just referred to in verse 15.

Paul here affirms that all of the Old Testament writings are *theopneustos*, "breathed out by God." Since it is *writings* that are said to be "breathed out," this breathing must be understood as a metaphor for speaking the words of Scripture. This verse thus states in

---

[2]See Wayne Grudem, *The Gift of Prophecy in 1 Corinthians* (Lanham, Md.: University Press of America, 1982), pp. 12–13; also Wayne Grudem, "Scripture's Self-Attestation," in *Scripture and Truth*, ed. D. A. Carson and J. Woodbridge, pp. 21–22.

[3]Some have suggested an alternative translation, namely, "Every God-breathed Scripture is also profitable for teaching. . . ." However, this translation is highly unlikely because it makes the *kai* ("also") extremely awkward in the Greek sentence. In coherent speech, one must say that something that has one characteristic before saying that it "also" has another characteristic. The "also" must indicate an addition to something that has previously been predicated. Thus, *theopneustos* ("God-breathed") and *ōphelimos* ("profitable") are both

best understood as predicate adjectives, and the best translation is, "All Scripture is God-breathed and is profitable for teaching. . . ."

[4]In at least two cases, 1 Tim. 5:18 and 2 Peter 3:16, *graphē* also includes some of the New Testament writings along with the Old Testament writings that it is referring to (see discussion below).

[5]I assume Pauline authorship of 1 and 2 Timothy and Titus throughout this book. For recent arguments defending Pauline authorship see George W. Knight III, *The Pastoral Epistles*, NIGTC (Grand Rapids: Eerdmans, and Carlisle: Paternoster, 1992), pp. 4–54.

brief form what was evident in many passages in the Old Testament: the Old Testament writings are regarded as God's Word in written form. For every word of the Old Testament, God is the one who spoke (and still speaks) it, although God used human agents to write these words down.[6]

A similar indication of the character of all Old Testament writings as God's words is found in 2 Peter 1:21. Speaking of the prophecies of Scripture (v. 20), which means at least the Old Testament Scriptures to which Peter encourages his readers to give careful attention (v. 19), Peter says that none of these prophecies ever came "by the impulse of man," but that "men moved by the Holy Spirit spoke from God." It is not Peter's intention to deny completely human volition or personality in the writing of Scripture (he says that the men "spoke"), but rather to say that the ultimate source of every prophecy was never a man's decision about what he wanted to write, but rather the Holy Spirit's action in the prophet's life, carried out in ways unspecified here (or, in fact, elsewhere in Scripture). This indicates a belief that all of the Old Testament prophecies (and, in light of vv. 19–20, this probably includes all of the written Scripture of the Old Testament) are spoken "from God": that is, they are God's own words.

Many other New Testament passages speak in similar ways about sections of the Old Testament. In Matthew 1:22, Isaiah's words in Isaiah 7:14 are cited as "what *the Lord had spoken* by the prophet." In Matthew 4:4 Jesus says to the devil, "Man shall not live by bread alone, but by *every word that proceeds from the mouth of God*." In the context of Jesus' repeated citations from Deuteronomy to answer every temptation, the words that proceed "from the mouth of God" are the written Scriptures of the Old Testament.

In Matthew 19:5, the words of the author in Genesis 2:24, not attributed to God in the Genesis narrative, are quoted by Jesus as words that God "said." In Mark 7:9–13, the same Old Testament passage can be called interchangeably "the commandment of God," or what "Moses said," or "the word of God." In Acts 1:16, the words of Psalms 69 and 109 are said to be words which "*the Holy Spirit spoke* beforehand by the mouth of David." Words of Scripture are thus said to be spoken by the Holy Spirit. In Acts 2:16–17, in quoting "what was spoken by the prophet Joel" in Joel 2:28–32, Peter inserts "*God declares*," thus attributing to God words written by Joel, and claiming that God is presently saying them.

Many other passages could be cited (see Luke 1:70; 24:25; John 5:45–47; Acts 3:18, 21; 4:25; 13:47; 28:25; Rom. 1:2; 3:2; 9:17; 1 Cor. 9:8–10; Heb. 1:1–2, 6–7), but the pattern of attributing to God the words of Old Testament Scripture should be very clear. Moreover, in several places it is *all* of the words of the prophets or the words of the Old Testament Scriptures that are said to compel belief or to be from God (see Luke 24:25, 27, 44; Acts 3:18; 24:14; Rom. 15:4).

---

[6]Older systematic theologies used the words *inspired* and *inspiration* to speak of the fact that the words of Scripture are spoken by God. This terminology was based especially on an older translation of 2 Tim. 3:16, which said, "All scripture is given by inspiration of God..." (KJV). However, the word *inspiration* has such a weak sense in ordinary usage today (every poet or songwriter claims to be "inspired" to write, and even athletes are said to give "inspired" performances) that I have not used it in this text. I have preferred the NIV rendering of 2 Tim. 3:16, "God-breathed," and have used other expressions to say that the words of Scripture are God's very words. The older phrase "*plenary* inspiration" meant that all the words of Scripture are God's words (the word *plenary* means "full"), a fact that I affirm in this chapter without using the phrase.

But if Paul meant only the Old Testament writings when he spoke of "Scripture" in 2 Timothy 3:16, how can this verse apply to the New Testament writings as well? Does it say anything about the character of the New Testament writings? To answer that question, we must realize that the Greek word *graphē* ("scripture") was a technical term for the New Testament writers and had a very specialized meaning. Even though it is used fifty-one times in the New Testament, every one of those instances uses it to refer to the Old Testament writings, not to any other words or writings outside the canon of Scripture. Thus, everything that belonged in the category "scripture" had the character of being "God-breathed": its words were God's very words.

But at two places in the New Testament we see New Testament writings also being called "scripture" along with the Old Testament writings. As we noted in chapter 3, in 2 Peter 3:16, Peter shows not only an awareness of the existence of written epistles from Paul, but also a clear willingness to classify "all of his [Paul's] epistles" with "the other scriptures." This is an indication that very early in the history of the church all of Paul's epistles were considered to be God's written words in the same sense as the Old Testament texts were. Similarly, in 1 Timothy 5:18, Paul quotes Jesus' words as found in Luke 10:7 and calls them "scripture."[7]

These two passages taken together indicate that during the time of the writing of the New Testament documents there was an awareness that *additions* were being made to this special category of writings called "scripture," writings that had the character of being God's very words. Thus, once we establish that a New Testament writing belongs to the special category "scripture," then we are correct in applying 2 Timothy 3:16 to that writing as well, and saying that that writing also has the characteristic Paul attributes to "all scripture": it is "God-breathed," and all its words are the very words of God.

Is there further evidence that the New Testament writers thought of their own writings (not just the Old Testament) as being words of God? In some cases, there is. In 1 Corinthians 14:37, Paul says, "If any one thinks that he is a prophet, or spiritual, he should acknowledge that *what I am writing to you is a command of the Lord.*" Paul has here instituted a number of rules for church worship at Corinth and has claimed for them the status of "commands of the Lord," for the phrase translated "what I am writing to you" contains a plural relative pronoun in Greek (*ha*) and is more literally translated "*the things* I am writing to you are a command of the Lord."

One objection to seeing the words of New Testament writers as words of God is sometimes brought from 1 Corinthians 7:12, where Paul distinguishes his words from words of the Lord: "To the rest I say, not the Lord . . ." A proper understanding of this passage is gained from verses 25 and 40, however. In verse 25 Paul says he has no command of the Lord concerning the unmarried but will give his own opinion. This must mean that he had possession of *no earthly word that Jesus had spoken on this subject* and probably also that he had received no subsequent revelation about it from Jesus. This is unlike the situation in verse 10 where he could simply repeat the content of Jesus' earthly teaching, "that the wife should not separate from her husband" and "that the husband should not divorce his wife." Thus, verse 12 must mean that Paul has *no record of any earthly teaching*

---

[7]See chapter 3, pp. 47–48, for discussion of 2 Peter 3:16 and
1 Tim. 5:17–18.

*of Jesus* on the subject of a believer who is married to an unbelieving spouse. Therefore, Paul gives his own instructions: "To the rest *I say, not the Lord,* that if any brother has a wife who is an unbeliever, and she consents to live with him, he should not divorce her" (1 Cor. 7:12).

It is remarkable therefore that Paul can go on in verses 12–15 to give several specific ethical standards for the Corinthians. What gave him the right to make such moral commands? He said that he spoke as one "who by the Lord's mercy is trustworthy" (1 Cor. 7:25). He seems to imply here that his considered judgments were able to be placed on the same authoritative level as the words of Jesus. Thus, 1 Corinthians 7:12, "To the rest I say, not the Lord," is an amazingly strong affirmation of Paul's own authority: if he did not have any words of Jesus to apply to a situation, he would simply use his own words, for his own words had just as much authority as the words of Jesus!

Indications of a similar view of the New Testament writings are found in John 14:26 and 16:13, where Jesus promised that the Holy Spirit would bring all that he had said to the disciples' remembrance and would guide them into all the truth. This indicates a special superintending work of the Holy Spirit whereby the disciples would be able to remember and record without error all that Jesus had said. Similar indications are also found in 2 Peter 3:2; 1 Corinthians 2:13; 1 Thessalonians 4:15; and Revelation 22:18–19.

**2. We Are Convinced of the Bible's Claims to Be God's Words as We Read the Bible.** It is one thing to affirm that the Bible *claims* to be the words of God. It is another thing to be convinced that those claims are true. Our ultimate conviction that the words of the Bible are God's words comes only when the Holy Spirit speaks *in* and *through* the words of the Bible to our hearts and gives us an inner assurance that these are the words of our Creator speaking to us. Just after Paul has explained that his apostolic speech consists of words taught by the Holy Spirit (1 Cor. 2:13), he says, "The natural man does not receive the things[8] of the Spirit of God, for they are folly to him, and he is not able to understand them because they are spiritually discerned" (1 Cor. 2:14). Apart from the work of the Spirit of God, a person will not receive spiritual truths and in particular will not receive or accept the truth that the words of Scripture are in fact the words of God.

But for those in whom God's Spirit is working there is a recognition that the words of the Bible are the words of God. This process is closely analogous to that by which those who believed in Jesus knew that his words were true. He said, "My sheep hear my voice, and I know them, and they follow me" (John 10:27). Those who are Christ's sheep hear the words of their great Shepherd as they read the words of Scripture, and they are convinced that these words are in fact the words of their Lord.

It is important to remember that this conviction that the words of Scripture are the words of God does *not* come *apart from* the words of Scripture or *in addition to* the words of Scripture. It is not as if the Holy Spirit one day whispers in our ear, "Do you see that Bible sitting on your desk? I want you to know that the words of that Bible are God's words." It is rather as people read Scripture that they hear their Creator's voice speaking

---

[8]I have translated the verse "things of the Spirit of God" because the Greek text has only the neuter plural definite article (*ta*) used as a substantive, and no specific noun is given. Thus, the RSV translation "the *gifts* of the Spirit of God" is more restrictive in subject matter than the actual words would justify and is certainly not required by the context.

to them in the words of Scripture and realize that the book they are reading is unlike any other book, that it is indeed a book of God's own words speaking to their hearts.

**3. Other Evidence Is Useful but Not Finally Convincing.** The previous section is not meant to deny the validity of other kinds of arguments that may be used to support the claim that the Bible is God's words. It is helpful for us to learn that the Bible is historically accurate, that it is internally consistent, that it contains prophecies that have been fulfilled hundreds of years later, that it has influenced the course of human history more than any other book, that it has continued changing the lives of millions of individuals throughout its history, that through it people come to find salvation, that it has a majestic beauty and a profound depth of teaching unmatched by any other book, and that it claims hundreds of times over to be God's very words. All of these arguments and others are useful to us and remove obstacles that might otherwise come in the way of our believing Scripture. But all of these arguments taken individually or together cannot finally be convincing. As the Westminster Confession of Faith said in 1643–46,

> We may be moved and induced by the testimony of the Church to an high and reverent esteem of the Holy Scripture. And the heavenliness of the matter, the efficacy of the doctrine, the majesty of the style, the consent of all the parts, the scope of the whole (which is, to give all glory to God), the full discovery it makes of the only way of man's salvation, the many other incomparable excellencies, and the entire perfection thereof, are arguments whereby it doth abundantly evidence itself to be the Word of God: yet notwithstanding, our full persuasion and assurance of the infallible truth and divine authority thereof, is from the inward work of the Holy Spirit bearing witness by and with the Word in our hearts. (chap. 1, para. 5)

**4. The Words of Scripture Are Self-Attesting.** Thus, the words of Scripture are "self-attesting." They cannot be "proved" to be God's words by appeal to any higher authority. For if an appeal to some higher authority (say, historical accuracy or logical consistency) were used to prove that the Bible is God's Word, then the Bible itself would not be our highest or absolute authority: it would be subordinate in authority to the thing to which we appealed to prove it to be God's Word. If we ultimately appeal to human reason, or to logic, or to historical accuracy, or to scientific truth, as the authority by which Scripture is shown to be God's words, then we have assumed the thing to which we appealed to be a higher authority than God's words and one that is more true or more reliable.

**5. Objection: This Is a Circular Argument.** Someone may object that to say Scripture proves itself to be God's words is to use a circular argument: we believe that Scripture is God's Word because it claims to be that. And we believe its claims because Scripture is God's Word. And we believe that it is God's Word because it claims to be that, and so forth.

It should be admitted that this is a kind of circular argument. However, that does not make its use invalid, for all arguments for an absolute authority must ultimately appeal to that authority for proof: otherwise the authority would not be an absolute or highest authority. This problem is not unique to the Christian who is arguing for the authority of the Bible. Everyone either implicitly or explicitly uses some kind of circular argument when defending his or her ultimate authority for belief.

Although these circular arguments are not always made explicit and are sometimes hidden beneath lengthy discussions or are simply assumed without proof, arguments for an ultimate authority in their most basic form take on a similar circular appeal to that authority itself, as some of the following examples show:

> "My reason is my ultimate authority because it seems reasonable to me to make it so."
>
> "Logical consistency is my ultimate authority because it is logical to make it so."
>
> "The findings of human sensory experiences are the ultimate authority for discovering what is real and what is not, because our human senses have never discovered anything else: thus, human sense experience tells me that my principle is true."
>
> "I know there can be no ultimate authority because I do not know of any such ultimate authority."

In all of these arguments for an ultimate standard of truth, an absolute authority for what to believe, there is an element of circularity involved.[9]

How then does a Christian, or anyone else, choose among the various claims for absolute authorities? Ultimately the truthfulness of the Bible will commend itself as being far more persuasive than other religious books (such as the *Book of Mormon* or the *Qur'an*), or than any other intellectual constructions of the human mind (such as logic, human reason, sense experience, scientific methodology, etc.). It will be more persuasive because in the actual experience of life, all of these other candidates for ultimate authority are seen to be inconsistent or to have shortcomings that disqualify them, while the Bible will be seen to be fully in accord with all that we know about the world around us, about ourselves, and about God.

The Bible will commend itself as being persuasive in this way, that is, if we are thinking rightly about the nature of reality, our perception of it and of ourselves, and our perception of God. The trouble is that because of sin our perception and analysis of God and creation is faulty. Sin is ultimately irrational, and sin makes us think incorrectly about God and about creation. Thus, in a world free from sin, the Bible would commend itself convincingly to all people as God's Word. But because sin distorts people's perception of reality, they do not recognize Scripture for what it really is. Therefore it requires the work of the Holy Spirit, overcoming the effects of sin, to enable us to be persuaded that the Bible is indeed the Word of God and that the claims it makes for itself are true.

---

[9]This point has been made well by John M. Frame, "God and Biblical Language: Transcendence and Immanence," in *God's Inerrant Word*, ed. John Warwick Montgomery (Minneapolis: Bethany Fellowship, 1974), pp. 159–77. See also J. P. Moreland, "The Rationality of Belief in Inerrancy," *TrinJ* 7:1 (1986), 75–86, for a helpful discussion of the way we reach convictions about issues of major significance in our lives.

Thus, in another sense, the argument for the Bible as God's Word and our ultimate authority is *not* a typical circular argument. The process of persuasion is perhaps better likened to a spiral in which increasing knowledge of Scripture and increasingly correct understanding of God and creation tend to supplement one another in a harmonious way, each tending to confirm the accuracy of the other. This is not to say that our knowledge of the world around us serves as a higher authority than Scripture, but rather that such knowledge, if it is correct knowledge, continues to give greater and greater assurance and deeper conviction that the Bible is the only truly ultimate authority and that other competing claims for ultimate authority are false.

**6. This Does Not Imply Dictation From God as the Sole Means of Communication.**
The entire preceding part of this chapter has argued that all the words of the Bible are God's words. At this point a word of caution is necessary. The fact that all the words of Scripture are God's words should not lead us to think that God dictated every word of Scripture to the human authors.

When we say that all the words of the Bible are God's words, we are talking about the *result* of the process of bringing Scripture into existence. To raise the question of dictation is to ask about the *process* that led to that result or the manner by which God acted in order to ensure the result that he intended.[10] It must be emphasized that the Bible does not speak of only one type of process or one manner by which God communicated to the biblical authors what he wanted to be said. In fact, there is indication of *a wide variety of processes* God used to bring about the desired result.

A few scattered instances of dictation are explicitly mentioned in Scripture. When the apostle John saw the risen Lord in a vision on the island of Patmos, Jesus spoke to him as follows: "To the angel of the church in Ephesus *write . . .*" (Rev. 2:1); "And to the angel of the church in Smyrna *write . . .*" (Rev. 2:8); "And to the angel of the church in Pergamum *write . . .*" (Rev. 2:12). These are examples of dictation pure and simple. The risen Lord tells John what to write, and John writes the words he hears from Jesus.

Something akin to this process is probably also seen occasionally in the Old Testament prophets. We read in Isaiah, "Then the word of the Lord came to Isaiah: 'Go and say to Hezekiah, Thus says the Lord, the God of David your father: I have heard your prayer, I have seen your tears; behold, I will add fifteen years to your life. I will deliver you and this city out of the hand of the king of Assyria, and defend this city'" (Isa. 38:4–6). The picture given us in this narrative is that Isaiah heard (whether with his physical ear or with a very forceful impression made upon his mind is difficult to say) the words God wanted him to say to Hezekiah, and Isaiah, acting as God's messenger, then took those words and *spoke* them as he had been instructed.

But in many other sections of Scripture such direct dictation from God is certainly not the manner by which the words of Scripture were caused to come into being. The author of Hebrews says that God spoke to our fathers by the prophets "in many and

---

[10]In some systematic theologies, this process by which God used human authors to write his very words is called "the mode of inspiration." I have not used this terminology in this book, since it does not seem to be a readily understandable phrase today.

various ways" (Heb. 1:1). On the opposite end of the spectrum from dictation we have, for instance, Luke's ordinary historical research for writing his gospel. He says:

> Inasmuch as many have undertaken to compile a narrative of the things which have been accomplished among us, just as they were delivered to us by those who from the beginning were eyewitnesses and ministers of the word, it seemed good to me also, having followed all things closely for some time past, to write an orderly account for you, most excellent Theophilus. . . . (Luke 1:1–3)

This is clearly not a process of dictation. Luke used ordinary processes of speaking to eyewitnesses and gathering historical data in order that he might write an accurate account of the life and teachings of Jesus. He did his historical research thoroughly, listening to the reports of many eyewitnesses and evaluating his evidence carefully. The gospel he wrote emphasizes what he thought important to emphasize and reflects his own characteristic style of writing.

In between these two extremes of dictation pure and simple on the one hand, and ordinary historical research on the other hand, we have many indications of various ways by which God communicated with the human authors of Scripture. In some cases Scripture gives us hints of these various processes: it speaks of dreams, of visions, of hearing the Lord's voice or standing in the council of the Lord; it also speaks of men who were with Jesus and observed his life and listened to his teaching, men whose memory of these words and deeds was made completely accurate by the working of the Holy Spirit as he brought things to their remembrance (John 14:26). Yet in many other cases the manner used by God to bring about the result that the words of Scripture were his words is simply not disclosed to us. Apparently many different methods were used, but it is not important that we discover precisely what these were in each case.

In cases where the ordinary human personality and writing style of the author were prominently involved, as seems the case with the major part of Scripture, all that we are able to say is that God's providential oversight and direction of the life of each author was such that their personalities, their backgrounds and training, their abilities to evaluate events in the world around them, their access to historical data, their judgment with regard to the accuracy of information, and their individual circumstances when they wrote,[11] were all exactly what God wanted them to be, so that when they actually came to the point of putting pen to paper, the words were fully their own words but also fully the words that God wanted them to write, words that God would also claim as his own.

## B. Therefore to Disbelieve or Disobey Any Word of Scripture Is to Disbelieve or Disobey God

The preceding section has argued that all the words in Scripture are God's words. Consequently, to disbelieve or disobey any word of Scripture is to disbelieve or disobey

---

[11]This would also include even the influence of a secretary (technically called an amanuensis) on the wording of a book: see the greeting from Tertius in Rom. 16:22.

God himself. Thus, Jesus can rebuke his disciples for not believing the Old Testament Scriptures (Luke 24:25). Believers are to keep or obey the disciples' words (John 15:20: "If they kept my word, they will keep yours also"). Christians are encouraged to remember "the commandment of the Lord and Savior through your apostles" (2 Peter 3:2). To disobey Paul's writings was to make oneself liable to church discipline, such as excommunication (2 Thess. 3:14) and spiritual punishment (2 Cor. 13:2−3), including punishment from God (this is the apparent sense of the passive verb "he is not recognized" in 1 Cor. 14:38). By contrast, God delights in everyone who "trembles" at his word (Isa. 66:2).

Throughout the history of the church the greatest preachers have been those who have recognized that they have no authority in themselves and have seen their task as being to explain the words of Scripture and apply them clearly to the lives of their hearers. Their preaching has drawn its power not from the proclamation of their own Christian experiences or the experiences of others, nor from their own opinions, creative ideas, or rhetorical skills, but from God's powerful words.[12] Essentially they stood in the pulpit, pointed to the biblical text, and said in effect to the congregation, "This is what this verse means. Do you see that meaning here as well? Then you must believe it and obey it with all your heart, for God himself, your Creator and your Lord, is saying this to you today!" Only the written words of Scripture can give this kind of authority to preaching.

## C. The Truthfulness of Scripture

**1. God Cannot Lie or Speak Falsely.** The essence of the authority of Scripture is its ability to compel us to believe and to obey it and to make such belief and obedience equivalent to believing and obeying God himself. Because this is so, it is needful to consider the truthfulness of Scripture, since to believe all the words of Scripture implies confidence in the complete truthfulness of the Scripture that we believe. Although this issue will be dealt with more fully when we consider the inerrancy of Scripture (see chapter 5), a brief treatment is given here.

Since the biblical writers repeatedly affirm that the words of the Bible, though human, are God's own words, it is appropriate to look at biblical texts that talk about *the character of God's words* and to apply these to the character of the words of Scripture. Specifically, there are a number of biblical passages that talk about the truthfulness of God's speech. Titus 1:2 speaks of "God, who never lies," or (more literally translated), "the unlying God." Because God is a God who cannot speak a "lie," his words can always be trusted. Since all of Scripture is spoken by God, all of Scripture must be "unlying," just as God himself is: there can be no untruthfulness in Scripture.[13]

---

[12]I am not denying that good speaking ability or creativity or telling of personal experiences have a place in preaching, for good preaching will include all of these (see Prov. 16:21, 23). I am saying that the power to change lives must come from the Word itself, and it will be evident to the hearers when a preacher really believes this.

[13]Some scholars object that it is "too simplistic" to argue as follows: "The Bible is God's words. God never lies. Therefore the Bible never lies." Yet it is precisely that kind of argument that Paul uses in Titus 1:2. He refers to the promises of eternal life made "ages ago" in Scripture and says the promises were made by God "who never lies." He thus calls on the

Hebrews 6:18 mentions two unchangeable things (God's oath and his promise) "in which *it is impossible for God to lie* (author's translation)." Here the author says not merely that God does not lie, but that it is not possible for him to lie. Although the immediate reference is only to oaths and promises, if it is impossible for God to lie in these utterances, then certainly it is impossible for him ever to lie (for Jesus harshly rebukes those who tell the truth only when under oath: Matt. 5:33–37; 23:16–22). Similarly, David says to God, "You are God, and *your words are true*" (2 Sam. 7:28).

**2. Therefore All the Words in Scripture Are Completely True and Without Error in Any Part.** Since the words of the Bible are God's words, and since God cannot lie or speak falsely, it is correct to conclude that there is no untruthfulness or error in any part of the words of Scripture. We find this affirmed several places in the Bible. "The words of the LORD are *words that are pure,* silver refined in a furnace on the ground, purified seven times" (Ps. 12:6, author's translation). Here the psalmist uses vivid imagery to speak of the undiluted purity of God's words: there is no imperfection in them. Also in Proverbs 30:5, we read, "*Every word of God proves true;* he is a shield to those who take refuge in him." It is not just some of the words of Scripture that are true, but every word. In fact, God's Word is fixed in heaven for all eternity: "For ever, O LORD, *your word is firmly fixed in the heavens*" (Ps. 119:89). Jesus can speak of the eternal nature of his own words: "Heaven and earth will pass away, but my words will not pass away" (Matt. 24:35). God's speech is placed in marked contrast to all human speech, for "God is not man, that he should lie, or a son of man, that he should repent" (Num. 23:19). These verses affirm explicitly what was implicit in the requirement that we believe all of the words of Scripture, namely, that there is no untruthfulness or falsehood affirmed in any of the statements of the Bible.

**3. God's Words Are the Ultimate Standard of Truth.** In John 17 Jesus prays to the Father, "Sanctify them in the truth; *your word is truth*" (John 17:17). This verse is interesting because Jesus does not use the adjectives *alēthinos* or *alēthēs* ("true"), which we might have expected, to say, "Your word is true." Rather, he uses a noun, *alētheia* ("truth"), to say that God's Word is not simply "true," but it is truth itself.

The difference is significant, for this statement encourages us to think of the Bible not simply as being "true" in the sense that it conforms to some higher standard of truth, but rather to think of the Bible as being itself the final standard of truth. The Bible is God's Word, and God's Word is the ultimate definition of what is true and what is not true: God's Word is itself *truth*. Thus we are to think of the Bible as the ultimate standard of truth, the reference point by which every other claim to truthfulness is to be measured. Those assertions that conform with Scripture are "true" while those that do not conform with Scripture are not true.

What then is truth? Truth is what God says, and we have what God says (accurately but not exhaustively) in the Bible.

---

truthfulness of God's own speech to prove the truthfulness of the words of Scripture. A "simple" argument this may be, but it is scriptural, and it is true. We should therefore not hesitate to accept it and use it.

**4. Might Some New Fact Ever Contradict the Bible?** Will any new scientific or historical fact ever be discovered that will contradict the Bible? Here we can say with confidence that this will never happen—it is in fact impossible. If any supposed "fact" is ever discovered that is said to contradict Scripture, then (if we have understood Scripture rightly) that "fact" must be false, because God, the author of Scripture, knows all true facts (past, present, and future). No fact will ever turn up that God did not know about ages ago and take into account when he caused Scripture to be written. Every true fact is something that God has known already from all eternity and is something that therefore cannot contradict God's speech in Scripture.

Nevertheless, it must be remembered that scientific or historical study (as well as other kinds of study of creation) can cause us to reexamine Scripture to see if it really teaches what we thought it taught. The Bible certainly does not teach that the earth was created in the year 4004 B.C., as some once thought (for the genealogical lists in Scripture have gaps in them). Yet it was in part historical, archaeological, astronomical, and geological study that caused Christians to reexamine Scripture to see if it really taught such a recent origin for the earth. Careful analysis of the biblical text showed that it did not teach this.

Similarly, the Bible does not teach that the sun goes around the earth, for it only uses descriptions of phenomena as we see them from our vantage point and does not purport to be describing the workings of the universe from some arbitrary "fixed" point somewhere out in space. Yet until the study of astronomy advanced enough to demonstrate the rotation of the earth on its axis, people *assumed* that the Bible taught that the sun goes around the earth. Then the study of scientific data prompted a reexamination of the appropriate biblical texts. Thus, whenever confronted with some "fact" that is said to contradict Scripture, we must not only examine the data adduced to demonstrate the fact in question; we must also reexamine the appropriate biblical texts to see if the Bible really teaches what we thought it to teach.

We should never fear but always welcome any new facts that may be discovered in any legitimate area of human research or study. For example, discoveries by archaeologists working in Syria have brought to light the Ebla Tablets. These extensive written records from the period around 2000 B.C. will eventually throw great light on our understanding of the world of the patriarchs and the events connected with the lives of Abraham, Isaac, and Jacob. Should Christians entertain any lingering apprehension that the publication of such data will prove some fact in Genesis to be incorrect? Certainly not! We should eagerly anticipate the publication of all such data with the absolute confidence that if it is correctly understood it will all be consistent with Scripture and will all confirm the accuracy of Scripture. No true fact will ever contradict the words of the God who knows all facts and who never lies.

## D. Written Scripture Is Our Final Authority

It is important to realize that the final form in which Scripture remains authoritative is its *written* form. It was the words of God *written* on the tablets of stone that Moses deposited in the ark of the covenant. Later, God commanded Moses and subsequent prophets to write their words in a book. And it was *written* Scripture (*graphē*) that Paul said was "God-breathed" (2 Tim. 3:16). Similarly, it is Paul's *writings* that are "a command of the Lord" (1 Cor. 14:37) and that could be classified with "the other scriptures" (2 Peter 3:16).

This is important because people sometimes (intentionally or unintentionally) attempt to substitute some other final standard than the written words of Scripture. For example, people will sometimes refer to "what Jesus really said" and claim that when we translate the Greek words of the Gospels back into the Aramaic language Jesus spoke, we can gain a better understanding of Jesus' words than was given by the writers of the Gospels. In fact, it is sometimes said that this work of reconstructing Jesus' words in Aramaic enables us to correct the erroneous translations made by the gospel authors.

In other cases, people have claimed to know "what Paul really thought" even when that is different from the meaning of the words he wrote. Or they have spoken of "what Paul should have said if he had been consistent with the rest of his theology." Similarly, others have spoken of "the church situation to which Matthew was writing" and have attempted to give normative force either to that situation or to the solution they think Matthew was attempting to bring about in that situation.

In all of these instances we must admit that asking about the words or situations that lie "behind" the text of Scripture may at times be helpful to us in understanding what the text means. Nevertheless, our hypothetical reconstructions of these words or situations can never replace or compete with Scripture itself as the final authority, nor should we ever allow them to contradict or call into question the accuracy of any of the words of Scripture. We must continually remember that we have in the Bible God's very words, and we must not try to "improve" on them in some way, for this cannot be done. Rather, we should seek to understand them and then trust them and obey them with our whole heart.

## QUESTIONS FOR PERSONAL APPLICATION

1. If you want to persuade someone that the Bible is God's Word, what do you want that person to read more than any other piece of literature?

2. Who would try to make people want to disbelieve something in Scripture? To disobey something in Scripture? Is there anything in the Bible that you do not want to believe? To obey? If your answers to either of the preceding two questions were positive, what is the best way to approach and to deal with the desires you have in this area?

3. Do you know of any proven fact in all of history that has shown something in the Bible to be false? Can the same be said about other religious writings such as the *Book of Mormon* or the *Qur'an*? If you have read in other books such as these, can you describe the spiritual effect they had on you? Compare that with the spiritual effect that reading the Bible has on you. Can you say that when you read the Bible you hear the voice of your Creator speaking to you in a way that is true of no other book?

4. Do you ever find yourself believing something not because you have external evidence for it but simply because it is written in Scripture? Is that proper faith, accord-

ing to Hebrews 11:1? If you do believe things simply because Scripture says them, what do you think Christ will say to you about this habit when you stand before his judgment seat? Do you think that trusting and obeying everything that Scripture affirms will ever lead you into sin or away from God's blessing in your life?

## SPECIAL TERMS

| | |
|---|---|
| absolute authority | inspiration |
| authority | plenary inspiration |
| circular argument | Scripture |
| dictation | self-attesting |
| God-breathed | |

## BIBLIOGRAPHY

Carson, D. A., and John Woodbridge, eds. *Hermeneutics, Authority, and Canon.* Grand Rapids: Zondervan, 1986.

_____. *Scripture and Truth.* Grand Rapids: Zondervan, 1983.

Geisler, Norman L., ed. *Inerrancy.* Grand Rapids: Zondervan, 1980.

Grudem, Wayne A. *The Gift of Prophecy in 1 Corinthians.* Washington, D.C.: University Press of America, 1982, pp. 1–54.

Helm, Paul. *The Divine Revelation: The Basic Issues.* Westchester, Ill.: Crossway, 1982.

Henry, Carl F. H. "Bible, Inspiration of." In *EDT,* pp. 145–49.

Kuyper, Abraham. *Principles of Sacred Theology.* Trans. by J. H. de Vries. Repr. ed.: Grand Rapids: Eerdmans, 1968, pp. 413–563 (first published as *Encyclopedia of Sacred Theology* in 1898).

Montgomery, John W., ed. *God's Inerrant Word.* Minneapolis: Bethany Fellowship, 1974.

Nash, Ronald H. *The Word of God and the Mind of Man.* Grand Rapids: Zondervan, 1982.

Packer, J. I. *"Fundamentalism" and the Word of God.* London: Inter-Varsity Press, 1958.

_____. "Infallibility and Inerrancy of the Bible." In *NDT,* pp. 337–39.

_____. "Scripture." In *NDT,* pp. 627–31.

Pinnock, Clark. *Biblical Revelation.* Chicago: Moody, 1971.

Radmacher, Earl D., and Robert D. Preus, eds. *Hermeneutics, Inerrancy, and the Bible.* Grand Rapids: Zondervan, 1984.

Van Til, Cornelius. *In Defense of the Faith,* vol. 1: *The Doctrine of Scripture.* Ripon, Calif.: den Dulk Christian Foundation, 1967.

_____. *In Defense of the Faith,* vol. 5: *An Introduction to Systematic Theology.* Phillipsburg, N.J.: Presbyterian and Reformed, 1976, pp. 110–58.

Warfield, B. B. *Limited Inspiration.* Philadelphia: Presbyterian and Reformed, 1962.

Wells, Paul. *James Barr and the Bible: Critique of a New Liberalism.* Phillipsburg, N.J.: Presbyterian and Reformed, 1980.

Wenham, John W. *Christ and the Bible.* London: Tyndale Press, 1972.

Woodbridge, John. *Biblical Authority: A Critique of the Rogers/McKim Proposal.* Grand Rapids: Zondervan, 1982.

Westminster Seminary Faculty. *The Infallible Word.* 3d ed. Philadelphia: Presbyterian and Reformed, 1967.

Young, Edward J. *Thy Word Is Truth.* Grand Rapids: Eerdmans, 1957.

### Works From a Noninerrancy Perspective

Baillie, John. *The Idea of Revelation in Recent Thought.* New York: Columbia University Press, 1956.

Barr, James. *Fundamentalism.* London: SCM, 1977.

Beegle, Dewey M. *Scripture, Tradition, and Infallibility.* Grand Rapids: Eerdmans, 1973.

Berkouwer, G. C. *Holy Scripture.* Trans. by Jack B. Rogers. Grand Rapids: Eerdmans, 1975.

Burtchaell, James Tunstead. *Catholic Theories of Biblical Inspiration Since 1810: A Review and Critique.* Cambridge: University Press, 1969.

Davis, Stephen T. *The Debate About the Bible.* Philadelphia: Westminster, 1977.

McKim, Donald K., ed. *The Authoritative Word: Essays on the Nature of Scripture.* Grand Rapids: Eerdmans, 1983.

Pinnock, Clark. *The Scripture Principle.* San Francisco: Harper and Row, 1984.

Rogers, Jack, ed. *Biblical Authority.* Waco, Tex.: Word, 1977.

Rogers, Jack, and Donald K. McKim. *The Authority and Interpretation of the Bible: An Historical Approach.* San Francisco: Harper and Row: 1979.

Vawter, Bruce. *Biblical Inspiration.* Philadelphia: Westminster, 1972 (a recent Roman Catholic work).

## SCRIPTURE MEMORY PASSAGE

**2 Timothy 3:16:** *All scripture is inspired by God and profitable for teaching, for reproof, for correction, and for training in righteousness.*

## HYMN

### "Standing on the Promises"

This hymn speaks of the promises of God's Word as the eternally firm and unchanging foundation on which we can rest our faith. In the midst of doubt and fear these promises "cannot fail." By standing firm on them we will be able to sing "Glory in the highest!" for all eternity. Yet the hymn speaks not merely of the promises of God's Word, but of all the contents of Scripture: the Bible is "the living Word of God" by which we "prevail" in the midst of adversity (v. 2), and it is the "Spirit's sword" by which we may be "overcoming daily" (v. 3). There is no other sure foundation on which to rest our faith than on the very words and promises of God. "I am standing on the promises of God!" is the joyful exclamation of a heart filled with faith, and it shall be our song throughout eternity.

Standing on the promises of Christ my King,
Through eternal ages let his praises ring!
Glory in the highest I will shout and sing
Standing on the promises of God!

*Chorus:*
Standing, standing, standing on the promises of God my Savior;
Standing, standing, I'm standing on the promises of God.

Standing on the promises that cannot fail
When the howling storms of doubt and fear assail;
By the living Word of God I shall prevail
Standing on the promises of God!

Standing on the promises of Christ the Lord,
Bound to him eternally by love's strong cord,
Overcoming daily with the Spirit's sword
Standing on the promises of God!

Standing on the promises I cannot fall,
List'ning every moment to the Spirit's call,
Resting in my Savior as my all in all
Standing on the promises of God!

AUTHOR: R. KELSO CARTER, 1886

# Chapter 5

# THE INERRANCY OF SCRIPTURE

## *Are there any errors in the Bible?*

Most books on systematic theology have not included a separate chapter on the inerrancy of the Bible. The subject has usually been dealt with under the heading of the authority of Scripture, and no further treatment has been considered necessary. However, this issue of inerrancy is of such concern in the evangelical world today that it warrants a separate chapter following our treatment of the authority of the Word of God.

## EXPLANATION AND SCRIPTURAL BASIS

### A. The Meaning of Inerrancy

We will not at this point repeat the arguments concerning the authority of Scripture that were given in chapter 4. There it was argued that all the words in the Bible are God's words, and that therefore to disbelieve or disobey any word in Scripture is to disbelieve or disobey God. It was argued further that the Bible clearly teaches that God cannot lie or speak falsely (2 Sam. 7:28; Titus 1:2; Heb. 6:18). Therefore, all the words in Scripture are claimed to be completely true and without error in any part (Num. 23:19; Pss. 12:6; 119:89, 96; Prov. 30:5; Matt. 24:35). God's words are, in fact, the ultimate standard of truth (John 17:17).

Especially relevant at this point are those Scripture texts that indicate the total truthfulness and reliability of God's words. "*The words of the LORD are words that are pure, silver refined in a furnace on the ground, purified seven times*" (Ps. 12:6, author's translation), indicates the absolute reliability and purity of Scripture. Similarly, "*Every word of God proves true; he is a shield to those who take refuge in him*" (Prov. 30:5), indicates the truthfulness of every word that God has spoken. Though error and at least partial falsehood may characterize the speech of every human being, it is the characteristic of God's speech even when spoken through sinful human beings that it is never false and that it never affirms error: "God is not man, that he should lie, or a son of man, that he should repent" (Num. 23:19) was spoken by sinful Balaam specifically about the prophetic words that God had spoken through his own lips.

With evidence such as this we are now in a position to define biblical inerrancy: *The inerrancy of Scripture means that Scripture in the original manuscripts does not affirm anything that is contrary to fact.*

This definition focuses on the question of truthfulness and falsehood in the language of Scripture. The definition in simple terms just means that *the Bible always tells the truth,* and that it always tells the truth *concerning everything it talks about.* This definition does not mean that the Bible tells us every fact there is to know about any one subject, but it affirms that what it does say about any subject is *true.*

It is important to realize at the outset of this discussion that the focus of this controversy is on the question of truthfulness in speech. It must be recognized that absolute truthfulness in speech is consistent with some other types of statements, such as the following:

**1. The Bible Can Be Inerrant and Still Speak in the Ordinary Language of Everyday Speech.** This is especially true in "scientific" or "historical" descriptions of facts or events. The Bible can speak of the sun rising and the rain falling because from the perspective of the speaker this is exactly what happens. From the standpoint of an observer standing on the sun (were that possible) or on some hypothetical "fixed" point in space, the earth rotates and brings the sun into view, and rain does not fall downward but upward or sideways or whatever direction necessary for it to be drawn by gravity toward the surface of the earth. But such explanations are hopelessly pedantic and would make ordinary communication impossible. From the standpoint of the speaker, the sun *does* rise and the rain *does* fall, and these are perfectly true descriptions of the natural phenomena the speaker observes.

A similar consideration applies to numbers when used in measuring or in counting. A reporter can say that 8,000 men were killed in a certain battle without thereby implying that he has counted everyone and that there are not 7,999 or 8,001 dead soldiers. If roughly 8,000 died, it would of course be false to say that 16,000 died, but it would not be false in most contexts for a reporter to say that 8,000 men died when in fact 7,823 or 8,242 had died: the limits of truthfulness would depend on the degree of precision implied by the speaker and expected by his original hearers.

This is also true for measurements. Whether I say, "I don't live far from my office," or "I live a little over a mile from my office," or "I live one mile from my office," or "I live 1.287 miles from my office," all four statements are still approximations to some degree of accuracy. Further degrees of accuracy might be obtained with more precise scientific instruments, but these would still be approximations to a certain degree of accuracy. Thus, measurements also, in order to be true, should conform to the degree of precision implied by the speaker and expected by the hearers in the original context. It should not trouble us, then, to affirm both that the Bible is absolutely truthful in everything it says and that it uses ordinary language to describe natural phenomena or to give approximations or round numbers when those are appropriate in the context.

We should also note that language can make vague or imprecise statements without being untrue. "I live a little over a mile from my office" is a vague and imprecise statement, but it is also inerrant: there is nothing untrue about it. It does not affirm anything that is contrary to fact. In a similar way, biblical statements can be imprecise and still be totally true. Inerrancy has to do with *truthfulness,* not with the degree of precision with which events are reported.

**2. The Bible Can Be Inerrant and Still Include Loose or Free Quotations.** The method by which one person quotes the words of another person is a procedure that in large part varies from culture to culture. In contemporary American and British culture we are used to quoting a person's exact words when we enclose the statement in quotation marks (this is called direct quotation). But when we use indirect quotation (with no quotation marks) we only expect an accurate report of the substance of a statement. Consider this sentence: "Elliot said that he would return home for supper right away." The sentence does not quote Elliot directly, but it is an acceptable and truthful report of Elliot's actual statement to his father, "I will come to the house to eat in two minutes," even though the indirect quotation included none of the speaker's original words.

Written Greek at the time of the New Testament had no quotation marks or equivalent kinds of punctuation, and an accurate citation of another person needed to include only a correct representation of the *content* of what the person said (rather like our indirect quotations): it was not expected to cite each word exactly. Thus, inerrancy is consistent with loose or free quotations of the Old Testament or of the words of Jesus, for example, so long as the *content* is not false to what was originally stated. The original writer did not ordinarily imply that he was using the exact words of the speaker and only those, nor did the original hearers expect verbatim quotation in such reporting.

**3. It Is Consistent With Inerrancy to Have Unusual or Uncommon Grammatical Constructions in the Bible.** Some of the language of Scripture is elegant and stylistically excellent. Other scriptural writings contain the rough-hewn language of ordinary people. At times this includes a failure to follow the commonly accepted "rules" of grammatical expression (such as the use of a plural verb where grammatical rules would require a singular verb, or the use of a feminine adjective where a masculine one would be expected, or different spelling for a word than the one commonly used, etc.). These stylistically or grammatically irregular statements (which are especially found in the book of Revelation) should not trouble us, for they do not affect the truthfulness of the statements under consideration: a statement can be ungrammatical but still be entirely true. For example, an uneducated backwoodsman in some rural area may be the most trusted man in the county even though his grammar is poor, because he has earned a reputation for never telling a lie. Similarly, there are a few statements in Scripture (in the original languages) that are ungrammatical (according to current standards of proper grammar at that time) but still inerrant because they are completely true. The issue is *truthfulness* in speech.

## B. Some Current Challenges to Inerrancy

In this section we examine the major objections that are commonly made against the concept of inerrancy.

**1. The Bible Is Only Authoritative for "Faith and Practice."** One of the most frequent objections is raised by those who say that the purpose of Scripture is to teach us in areas that concern "faith and practice" only; that is, in areas that directly relate to our religious faith or to our ethical conduct. This position would allow for the possibility of false statements in Scripture, for example, in *other* areas such as in minor historical details or scientific facts—these areas, it is said, do not concern the purpose of the Bible, which is to instruct us in what we should believe and how we are to live.[1] Its advocates often prefer to say that the Bible is "*infallible*," but they hesitate to use the word *inerrant*.[2]

The response to this objection can be stated as follows: the Bible repeatedly affirms that all of Scripture is profitable for us (2 Tim. 3:16) and that *all* of it is "God-breathed." Thus it is completely pure (Ps. 12:6), perfect (Ps. 119:96), and true (Prov. 30:5). The Bible itself does not make any restriction on the kinds of subjects to which it speaks truthfully.

The New Testament contains further affirmations of the reliability of all parts of Scripture: in Acts 24:14, Paul says that he worships God, "*believing everything* laid down by the law or written in the prophets." In Luke 24:25, Jesus says that the disciples are "foolish men" because they are "slow of heart to believe all that the prophets have spoken." In Romans 15:4, Paul says that "*whatever* was written" in the Old Testament was "written for our instruction." These texts give no indication that there is any part of Scripture that is not to be trusted or relied on completely. Similarly, in 1 Corinthians 10:11, Paul can refer even to minor historical details in the Old Testament (sitting down to eat and drink, rising up to dance) and can say both that they "*happened*" (thus implying historical reliability) and "were written down for our instruction."

If we begin to examine the way in which the New Testament authors trust the smallest historical details of the Old Testament narrative, we see no intention to separate out matters of "faith and practice," or to say that this is somehow a recognizable category of affirmations, or to imply that statements not in that category need not be trusted or thought to be inerrant. Rather, it seems that the New Testament authors are willing to cite and affirm as true *every detail* of the Old Testament.

In the following list are some examples of these historical details cited by New Testament authors. If all of these are matters of "faith and practice," then *every* historical detail of the Old Testament is a matter of "faith and practice," and this objection ceases to be an objection to inerrancy. On the other hand, if so many details can be affirmed, then it seems that all of the historical details in the Old Testament can be affirmed as true, and we should not speak of restricting the necessary truthfulness of Scripture to some category of "faith and practice" that would exclude certain minor details. There are no types of details left that could not be affirmed as true.

The New Testament gives us the following data: David ate the bread of the Presence (Matt. 12:3–4); Jonah was in the whale (Matt. 12:40); the men of Nineveh repented (Matt. 12:41); the queen of the South came to hear Solomon (Matt. 12:42); Elijah was

---

[1]A good defense of this position can be found in a collection of essays edited by Jack Rogers, *Biblical Authority* (Waco, Tex.: Word, 1977); and, more extensively, in Jack B. Rogers and Donald McKim, *The Authority and Interpretation of the Bible: An Historical Approach* (San Francisco: Harper and Row, 1979).

[2]Until about 1960 or 1965 the word *infallible* was used interchangeably with the word *inerrant*. But in recent years, at least in the United States, the word *infallible* has been used in a weaker sense to mean that the Bible will not lead us astray in matters of faith and practice.

sent to the widow of Zarephath (Luke 4:25–26); Naaman the Syrian was cleansed of leprosy (Luke 4:27); on the day Lot left Sodom fire and brimstone rained from heaven (Luke 17:29; cf. v. 32 with its reference to Lot's wife who turned to salt); Moses lifted up the serpent in the wilderness (John 3:14); Jacob gave a field to Joseph (John 4:5); many details of the history of Israel occurred (Acts 13:17–23); Abraham believed and received the promise before he was circumcised (Rom. 4:10); Abraham was about one hundred years old (Rom. 4:19); God told Rebekah before her children were born that the elder child would serve the younger (Rom. 9:10–12); Elijah spoke with God (Rom. 11:2–4); the people of Israel passed through the sea, ate and drank spiritual food and drink, desired evil, sat down to drink, rose up to dance, indulged in immorality, grumbled, and were destroyed (1 Cor. 10:11); Abraham gave a tenth of everything to Melchizedek (Heb. 7:1–2); the Old Testament tabernacle had a specific and detailed design (Heb. 9:1–5); Moses sprinkled the people and the tabernacle vessels with blood and water, using scarlet wool and hyssop (Heb. 9:19–21); the world was created by the Word of God (Heb. 11:3);[3] many details of the lives of Abel, Enoch, Noah, Abraham, Moses, Rahab, and others actually happened (Heb. 11, passim); Esau sold his birthright for a single meal and later sought it back with tears (Heb. 12:16–17); Rahab received the spies and sent them out another way (James 2:25); eight persons were saved in the ark (1 Peter 3:20; 2 Peter 2:5); God turned Sodom and Gomorrah to ashes but saved Lot (2 Peter 2:6–7); Balaam's donkey spoke (2 Peter 2:16).

This list indicates that the New Testament writers were willing to rely on the truthfulness of any part of the historical narratives of the Old Testament. No detail was too insignificant to be used for the instruction of New Testament Christians. There is no indication that they thought of a certain category of scriptural statements that were unreliable and untrustworthy (such as "historical and scientific" statements as opposed to doctrinal and moral passages). It seems clear that the Bible itself does not support any restriction on the kinds of subjects to which it speaks with absolute authority and truth; indeed, many passages in Scripture actually exclude the validity of this kind of restriction.

A second response to those who limit the necessary truthfulness of Scripture to matters of "faith and practice" is to note that this position mistakes the *major* purpose of Scripture for the *total* purpose of Scripture. To say that the major purpose of Scripture is to teach us in matters of "faith and practice" is to make a useful and correct summary of God's purpose in giving us the Bible. But as a *summary* it includes only the most prominent purpose of God in giving us Scripture. It is not, however, legitimate to use this summary to deny that it is *part* of the purpose of Scripture to tell us about minor historical details or about some aspects of astronomy or geography, and so forth. A summary cannot properly be used to deny one of the things it is summarizing! To use it this way would simply show that the summary is not detailed enough to specify the items in question.

---

[3]This is not a minor detail, but it is useful as an example of a "scientific" fact that is affirmed in the Old Testament and one about which the author says that we have knowledge "by faith"; thus, faith here is explicitly said to involve trust in the truthfulness of a scientific and historical fact recorded in the Old Testament.

It is better to say that the *whole purpose* of Scripture is to say everything it does say, on whatever subject. Every one of God's words in Scripture was deemed by him to be important for us. Thus, God issues severe warnings to anyone who would take away even one word from what he has said to us (Deut. 4:2; 12:32; Rev. 22:18–19): we cannot add to God's words or take from them, for all are part of his larger purpose in speaking to us. Everything stated in Scripture is there because God intended it to be there: God does not say anything unintentionally! Thus, this first objection to inerrancy makes a wrong use of a summary and thereby incorrectly attempts to impose artificial limits on the kinds of things about which God can speak to us.

**2. The Term *Inerrancy* Is a Poor Term.** People who make this second objection say that the term *inerrancy* is too precise and that in ordinary usage it denotes a kind of absolute scientific precision that we do not want to claim for Scripture. Furthermore, those who make this objection note that the term *inerrancy* is not used in the Bible itself. Therefore, it is probably an inappropriate term for us to insist upon.

The response to this objection may be stated as follows: first, the scholars who have used the term *inerrancy* have defined it clearly for over a hundred years, and they have always allowed for the "limitations" that attach to speech in ordinary language. In no case has the term been used to denote a kind of absolute scientific precision by any responsible representative of the inerrancy position. Therefore those who raise this objection to the term are not giving careful enough attention to the way in which it has been used in theological discussions for more than a century.

Second, it must be noted that we often use nonbiblical terms to summarize a biblical teaching. The word *Trinity* does not occur in Scripture, nor does the word *incarnation*. Yet both of these terms are very helpful because they allow us to summarize in one word a true biblical concept, and they are therefore helpful in enabling us to discuss a biblical teaching more easily.

It should also be noted that no other single word has been proposed which says as clearly what we want to affirm when we wish to talk about total truthfulness in language. The word *inerrancy* does this quite well, and there seems no reason not to continue to use it for that purpose.

Finally, in the church today we seem to be unable to carry on the discussion around this topic without the use of this term. People may object to this term if they wish, but, like it or not, this is the term about which the discussion has focused and almost certainly will continue to focus in the next several decades. When the International Council on Biblical Inerrancy (ICBI) in 1977 began a ten-year campaign to promote and defend the idea of biblical inerrancy, it became inevitable that this word would be the one about which discussion would proceed. The "Chicago Statement on Biblical Inerrancy," which was drafted and published in 1978 under ICBI sponsorship, defined what most evangelicals mean by inerrancy, perhaps not perfectly, but quite well, and further objections to such a widely used and well-defined term seem to be unnecessary and unhelpful for the church.

**3. We Have No Inerrant Manuscripts; Therefore, Talk About an Inerrant Bible Is Misleading.** Those who make this objection point to the fact that inerrancy has always been claimed for the first or *original copies of the biblical documents.*[4] Yet none of these survive: we have only copies of copies of what Moses or Paul or Peter wrote. What is the use, then, of placing so great importance on a doctrine that applies only to manuscripts that no one has?

In reply to this objection, it may first be stated that for over 99 percent of the words of the Bible, we *know* what the original manuscript said. Even for many of the verses where there are textual variants (that is, different words in different ancient copies of the same verse), the correct decision is often quite clear, and there are really very few places where the textual variant is both difficult to evaluate and significant in determining the meaning. In the small percentage of cases where there is significant uncertainty about what the original text said, the general sense of the sentence is usually quite clear from the context. (One does not have to be a Hebrew or Greek scholar to know where these variants are, because all modern English translations indicate them in marginal notes with words such as "some ancient manuscripts read . . ." or "other ancient authorities add. . . .")

This is not to say that the study of textual variants is unimportant, but it is to say that the study of textual variants has not left us in confusion about what the original manuscripts said.[5] It has rather brought us extremely close to the content of those original manuscripts. For most practical purposes, then, the *current published scholarly texts of the Hebrew Old Testament and Greek New Testament are the same as the original manuscripts.* Thus, when we say that the original manuscripts were inerrant, we are also implying that over 99 percent of the words in our present manuscripts are also inerrant, for they are exact copies of the originals. Furthermore, we *know* where the uncertain readings are (for where there are no textual variants we have no reason to expect faulty copying of the original).[6] Thus, our present manuscripts are for most purposes the same as the original manuscripts, and the doctrine of inerrancy therefore directly concerns our present manuscripts as well.

Furthermore, it is extremely important to affirm the inerrancy of the original documents, for the subsequent copies were made by men with no claim or guarantee by God that these copies would be perfect. But the original manuscripts are those to which the claims to be God's very words apply. Thus, if we have mistakes in the copies (as we do), then these are only the *mistakes of men.* But if we have mistakes in the *original manuscripts,* then we are forced to say not only that men made mistakes, but that *God himself* made a mistake and spoke falsely. This we cannot do.

---

[4] In theological terms, these original copies are called the "autographs," using the prefix *auto-,* meaning "self," and the root *graph,* meaning "writing," to refer to a copy written by the author himself.

[5] An excellent survey of the work of studying textual variants in the extant manuscripts of the New Testament is Bruce M. Metzger, *The Text of the New Testament: Its Transmission, Corruption, and Restoration,* 2d ed. (Oxford: Clarendon Press, 1968).

[6] Of course the theoretical possibility exists that there was a copying error in the very first copy made of one of Paul's epistles, for instance, and that this error has been reproduced in all remaining copies. But this must be thought unlikely because (1) it would require that only one copy was made of the original, or that only one copy was the basis for all other extant copies, and (2) our earlier argument about the faithfulness of God in preserving the canon (see chapter 3, p. 51) would seem to imply that if such a mistake did occur, it would not be one that would materially affect our understanding of Scripture. The existence of such a copying error cannot be either proven or disproven, but further speculation about it apart from hard evidence does not appear to be profitable.

**4. The Biblical Writers "Accommodated" Their Messages in Minor Details to the False Ideas Current in Their Day, and Affirmed or Taught Those Ideas in an Incidental Way.** This objection to inerrancy is slightly different from the one that would restrict the inerrancy of Scripture to matters of faith and practice, but it is related to it. Those who hold this position argue that it would have been very difficult for the biblical writers to communicate with the people of their time if they had tried to correct all the false historical and scientific information believed by their contemporaries. Those who hold this position would not argue that the points where the Bible affirms false information are numerous, or even that these places are the main points of any particular section of Scripture. Rather, they would say that when the biblical writers were attempting to make a larger point, they sometimes incidentally affirmed some falsehood believed by the people of their time.[7]

To this objection to inerrancy it can be replied, first, that God is Lord of human language who can use human language to communicate perfectly without having to affirm any false ideas that may have been held by people during the time of the writing of Scripture. This objection to inerrancy essentially denies God's effective lordship over human language.

Second, we must respond that such "accommodation" by God to our misunderstandings would imply that God had acted contrary to his character as an "unlying God" (Num. 23:19; Titus 1:2; Heb. 6:18). It is not helpful to divert attention from this difficulty by repeated emphasis on the gracious condescension of God to speak on our level. Yes, God does condescend to speak our language, the language of human beings. But no passage of Scripture teaches that he "condescends" so as to act contrary to his moral character. He is never said to be able to condescend so as to affirm—even incidentally—something that is false. If God were to "accommodate" himself in this way, he would cease to be the "unlying God." He would cease to be the God the Bible represents him to be. Such activity would not in any way show God's greatness, for God does not manifest his greatness by acting in a way that contradicts his character. This objection thus at root misunderstands the purity and unity of God as they affect all of his words and deeds.

Furthermore, such a process of accommodation, if it actually had occurred, would create a serious moral problem for us. We are to be imitators of God's moral character (Lev. 11:44; Luke 6:36; Eph. 5:1; 1 Peter 5:1, et al.). Paul says, since in our new natures we are becoming more like God (Eph. 4:24), we should "put away falsehood" and "speak the truth" with one another (v. 25). We are to imitate God's truthfulness in our speech. However, if the accommodation theory is correct, then God *intentionally* made incidental affirmations of falsehood in order to enhance communication. Therefore, would it not also be right for us intentionally to make incidental affirmations of falsehood whenever it would enhance communication? Yet this would be tantamount to saying that a minor falsehood told for a good purpose (a "white lie") is not wrong. Such a position, contradicted by the Scripture passages cited above concerning God's total truthfulness in speech, cannot be held to be valid.

---

[7]An explanation of this view can be found in Daniel P. Fuller, "Benjamin B. Warfield's View of Faith and History," *BETS* 11 (1968): 75–83.

**5. Inerrancy Overemphasizes the Divine Aspect of Scripture and Neglects the Human Aspect.** This more general objection is made by those who claim that people who advocate inerrancy so emphasize the divine aspect of Scripture that they downplay its human aspect.

It is agreed that Scripture has both a human and a divine aspect, and that we must give adequate attention to both. However, those who make this objection almost invariably go on to insist that the truly "human" aspects of Scripture *must* include the presence of some errors in Scripture. We can respond that though the Bible is fully human in that it was written by human beings using their own language, the activity of God in overseeing the writing of Scripture and causing it to be also his words means that it is different from much other human writing in precisely this aspect: it does not include error. That is exactly the point made even by sinful, greedy, disobedient Balaam in Numbers 23:19: God's speech through sinful human beings is different from the ordinary speech of men because "God is not man that he should lie." Moreover, it is simply not true that all human speech and writing contains error, for we make dozens of statements each day that are completely true. For example: "My name is Wayne Grudem." "I have three children." "I ate breakfast this morning."

**6. There Are Some Clear Errors in the Bible.** This final objection, that there are clear errors in the Bible, is either stated or implied by most of those who deny inerrancy, and for many of them the conviction that there are some actual errors in Scripture is a major factor in persuading them to challenge the doctrine of inerrancy.

In every case, the first answer that should be made to this objection is to ask where such errors are. In which specific verse or verses do these errors occur? It is surprising how frequently one finds that this objection is made by people who have little or no idea where the specific errors are, but who believe there are errors because others have told them so.

In other cases, however, people will mention one or more specific passages where, they claim, there is a false statement in Scripture. In these cases, it is important that we look at the biblical text itself, and look at it very closely. If we believe that the Bible is indeed inerrant, we should be eager and certainly not afraid to inspect these texts in minute detail. In fact, our expectation will be that close inspection will show there to be no error at all. Once again it is surprising how often it turns out that a careful reading just of the English text of the passage in question will bring to light one or more possible solutions to the difficulty.

In a few passages, no solution to the difficulty may be immediately apparent from reading the English text. At that point it is helpful to consult some commentaries on the text. Both Augustine (A.D. 354–430) and John Calvin (1509–64), along with many more recent commentators, have taken time to deal with most of the alleged "problem texts" and to suggest plausible solutions to them. Furthermore some writers have made collections of all the most difficult texts and have provided suggested answers for them.[8]

There are a few texts where a knowledge of Hebrew or Greek may be necessary to find a solution, and those who do not have firsthand access to these languages may have to find

---

[8]The interested reader may consult, for example, Gleason L. Archer, *Encyclopedia of Bible Difficulties* (Grand Rapids: Zondervan, 1982); William Arndt, *Does the Bible Contradict Itself?* (St. Louis: Concordia, 1955); idem., *Bible Difficulties*

answers either from a more technical commentary or by asking someone who does have this training. Of course, our understanding of Scripture is never perfect, and this means that there may be cases where we will be unable to find a solution to a difficult passage at the present time. This may be because the linguistic, historical, or contextual evidence we need to understand the passage correctly is presently unknown to us. This should not trouble us in a small number of passages so long as the overall pattern of our investigation of these passages has shown that there is, in fact, no error where one has been alleged.[9]

But while we must allow the *possibility* of being unable to solve a particular problem, it should also be stated that there are many evangelical Bible scholars today who will say that they do not presently know of any problem texts for which there is no satisfactory solution. It is possible, of course, that some such texts could be called to their attention in the future, but during the past fifteen years or so of controversy over biblical inerrancy, no such "unsolved" text has been brought to their attention.[10]

Finally, a historical perspective on this question is helpful. There are no really "new" problems in Scripture. The Bible in its entirety is over 1,900 years old, and the alleged "problem texts" have been there all along. Yet throughout the history of the church there has been a firm belief in the inerrancy of Scripture in the sense in which it is defined in this chapter. Moreover, for these hundreds of years highly competent biblical scholars have read and studied those problem texts and still have found no difficulty in holding to inerrancy. This should give us confidence that the solutions to these problems are available and that belief in inerrancy is entirely consistent with a lifetime of detailed attention to the text of Scripture.[11]

## C. Problems With Denying Inerrancy

The problems that come with a denial of biblical inerrancy are not insignificant, and when we understand the magnitude of these problems it gives us further encouragement not only to affirm inerrancy but also to affirm its importance for the church. Some of the more serious problems are listed here.

**1. If We Deny Inerrancy, a Serious Moral Problem Confronts Us: May We Imitate God and Intentionally Lie in Small Matters Also?** This is similar to the point made in response to objection #4, above, but here it applies not only to those who espouse objection #4 but also more broadly to all who deny inerrancy. Ephesians 5:1 tells us to be

---

(St. Louis: Concordia, 1932); and John W. Haley, *Alleged Discrepancies of the Bible* (1874; reprinted Grand Rapids: Baker, 1977). Almost all of the difficult texts have also received helpful analysis in the extensive notes to *The NIV Study Bible,* ed. Kenneth Barker et al. (Grand Rapids: Zondervan, 1985).

[9]J. P. Moreland, "The Rationality of Belief in Inerrancy," in *TrinJ* 7:1 (1986): 75–86, argues convincingly that Christians should not abandon the doctrine of inerrancy simply because of a small number of "problem texts" for which they presently have no clear solution.

[10]The present writer, for example, has during the last twenty years examined dozens of these "problem texts" that have been brought to his attention in the context of the inerrancy debate. In every one of those cases, upon close inspection of the text a plausible solution has become evident.

[11]On the history of inerrancy in the church, see the essays by Philip Hughes, Geoffrey W. Bromiley, W. Robert Godfrey, and John D. Woodbridge and Randall H. Balmer in *Scripture and Truth.* See also the more extensive study by John D. Woodbridge, *Biblical Authority: A Critique of the Rogers and McKim Proposal* (Grand Rapids: Zondervan, 1982).

imitators of God. But a denial of inerrancy that still claims that the words of Scripture are God-breathed words necessarily implies that God intentionally spoke falsely to us in some of the less central affirmations of Scripture. But if this is right for God to do, how can it be wrong for us? Such a line of reasoning would, if we believed it, exert strong pressure on us to begin to speak untruthfully in situations where that might seem to help us communicate better, and so forth. This position would be a slippery slope with ever-increasing negative results in our own lives.

**2. If Inerrancy Is Denied, We Begin to Wonder If We Can Really Trust God in Anything He Says.** Once we become convinced that God has spoken falsely to us in some minor matters in Scripture, then we realize that God is *capable* of speaking falsely to us. This will have a detrimental effect on our ability to take God at his word and trust him completely or obey him fully in the rest of Scripture. We will begin to disobey initially those sections of Scripture that we least wish to obey, and to distrust initially those sections that we are least inclined to trust. But such a procedure will eventually increase, to the great detriment of our spiritual lives. Of course, such a decline in trust and obedience to Scripture may not necessarily follow in the life of every individual who denies inerrancy, but this will certainly be the general pattern, and it will be the pattern exhibited over the course of a generation that is taught to deny inerrancy.

**3. If We Deny Inerrancy, We Essentially Make Our Own Human Minds a Higher Standard of Truth Than God's Word Itself.** We use our minds to pass judgment on some sections of God's Word and pronounce them to be in error. But this is in effect to say that we know truth more certainly and more accurately than God's Word does (or than God does), at least in these areas. Such a procedure, making our own minds to be a higher standard of truth than God's Word, is the root of all intellectual sin.[12]

**4. If We Deny Inerrancy, Then We Must Also Say That the Bible Is Wrong Not Only in Minor Details but in Some of Its Doctrines as Well.** A denial of inerrancy means that we say that the Bible's teaching about the *nature of Scripture* and about the *truthfulness and reliability of God's words* is also false. These are not minor details but are major doctrinal concerns in Scripture.[13]

## QUESTIONS FOR PERSONAL APPLICATION

1. Why do you think the debate about inerrancy has become such a large issue in this century? Why do people on both sides of the question think it to be important?

---

[12]See chapter 4, p. 68, for a discussion of the Bible as our absolute standard of truth.

[13]Although the undesirable positions listed above are logically related to a denial of inerrancy, a word of caution is in order: Not all who deny inerrancy will also adopt the undesirable conclusions just listed. Some people (probably inconsistently) will deny inerrancy but not take these next logical steps. In debates over inerrancy, as in other theological discussions, it is important that we criticize people on the basis of views they actually hold, and distinguish those views clearly from positions we think they would hold if they were consistent with their stated views.

2. If you thought there were some small errors affirmed by Scripture, how do you think that would affect the way you read Scripture? Would it affect your concern for truthfulness in everyday conversation?

3. Do you know of any Scripture texts that seem to contain errors? What are they? Have you tried to resolve the difficulties in those texts? If you have not found a solution to some text, what further steps might you try?

4. As Christians go through life learning to know their Bibles better and growing in Christian maturity, do they tend to trust the Bible more or less? In heaven, do you think you will believe the Bible is inerrant? If so, will you believe it more firmly or less firmly than you do now?

5. If you are convinced that the Bible teaches the doctrine of inerrancy, how do you feel about it? Are you glad that such a teaching is there, or do you feel it to be something of a burden which you would rather not have to defend?

6. Does belief in inerrancy guarantee sound doctrine and a sound Christian life? How can Jehovah's Witnesses say that the Bible is inerrant while they themselves have so many false teachings?

7. If you agree with inerrancy, do you think belief in inerrancy should be a requirement for church membership? For teaching a Sunday school class? For holding a church office such as elder or deacon? For being ordained as a pastor? For teaching at a theological seminary? Why or why not?

8. When there is a doctrinal controversy in the church, what are the personal dangers facing those whose position is more consistent with Scripture? In particular, how could pride in correct doctrine become a problem? What is the solution? Do you think inerrancy is an important issue for the future of the church? Why or why not? How do you think it will be resolved?

## SPECIAL TERMS

| | |
|---|---|
| autograph | inerrant |
| faith and practice | infallible |
| ICBI | textual variant |

## BIBLIOGRAPHY

(See also the bibliography for chapter 4, "Authority," much of which is also relevant here, but only part of which has been listed again.)

Archer, Gleason. *Encyclopedia of Bible Difficulties.* Grand Rapids: Zondervan, 1982.

Arndt, W. *Bible Difficulties.* St. Louis: Concordia, 1932.

_____. *Does the Bible Contradict Itself?* St. Louis: Concordia, 1955.

Boice, James, ed. *The Foundation of Biblical Authority.* Grand Rapids: Zondervan, 1978.

Carson, D. A., and John Woodbridge, eds. *Hermeneutics, Authority, and Canon.* Grand Rapids: Zondervan, 1986.

_____. *Scripture and Truth*. Grand Rapids: Zondervan, 1983.

Feinberg, Paul. "Bible, Inerrancy and Infallibility of." In *EDT*, pp. 141–45.

Geisler, Norman, ed. *Biblical Errancy: An Analysis of Its Philosophical Roots*. Grand Rapids: Zondervan, 1981.

_____. ed. *Inerrancy*. Grand Rapids: Zondervan, 1979 (papers from the October 1978 Chicago Conference of the ICBI).

Haley, John W. *Alleged Discrepancies of the Bible*. Repr. ed. Grand Rapids: Baker, 1977 (first published 1874).

Lindsell, Harold. *The Battle for the Bible*. Grand Rapids: Zondervan, 1976.

_____. *The Bible in the Balance*. Grand Rapids: Zondervan, 1979.

Montgomery, John W., ed. *God's Inerrant Word*. Minneapolis: Bethany Fellowship, 1974.

Packer, J. I. "Scripture." In *NDT*, pp. 627–31.

_____. "Infallibility and Inerrancy of the Bible." In *NDT*, 337–39.

Schaeffer, Francis. *No Final Conflict: The Bible Without Error in All That It Affirms*. Downers Grove, Ill.: InterVarsity Press, 1975.

Warfield, B. B. *Limited Inspiration*. Philadelphia: Presbyterian and Reformed, 1962.

Woodbridge, John. *Biblical Authority: A Critique of the Rogers/McKim Proposal*. Grand Rapids: Zondervan, 1982.

Young, Edward J. *Thy Word Is Truth*. Grand Rapids: Eerdmans, 1957.

**Works From a Noninerrancy Perspective**
(See also the bibliography for chapter 4.)

Barr, James. *Fundamentalism*. London: SCM, 1977.

Beegle, Dewey M. *Scripture, Tradition, and Infallibility*. Grand Rapids: Eerdmans, 1973.

Davis, Stephen T. *The Debate About the Bible*. Philadelphia: Westminster, 1977.

McKim, Donald K., ed. *The Authoritative Word: Essays on the Nature of Scripture*. Grand Rapids: Eerdmans, 1983.

Rogers, Jack, ed. *Biblical Authority*. Waco, Tex.: Word, 1977.

Rogers, Jack B., and Donald K. McKim. *The Authority and Interpretation of the Bible: An Historical Approach*. San Francisco: Harper and Row, 1979.

## SCRIPTURE MEMORY PASSAGE

**Psalm 12:6:** *The promises [literally, "words"] of the LORD are promises ["words"] that are pure, silver refined in a furnace on the ground, purified seven times.*

## HYMN

### "The Law of the Lord is Perfect"

This modern setting of Psalm 19:7–11 expresses the perfection of God's Word in several different ways and shows various aspects of its application to our lives.

The law of the Lord is perfect,
    converting the soul.
The testimony of the Lord is sure,
    making wise the simple.

Refrain:
More to be desired are they than gold,
    yea than much fine gold.
Sweeter also than honey
    and the honeycomb.

The statutes of the Lord are right,
    rejoicing the heart.
The commandments of the Lord are pure,
    enlight'ning the eyes.

The fear of the Lord is clean,
    enduring forever.
The judgments of the Lord are true,
    and righteous altogether.

AUTHOR: ANONYMOUS (FROM PS. 19:7–11)

# Chapter 6

# THE FOUR CHARACTERISTICS OF SCRIPTURE: (2) CLARITY

## *Can only Bible scholars understand the Bible rightly?*

## EXPLANATION AND SCRIPTURAL BASIS

Anyone who has begun to read the Bible seriously will realize that some parts can be understood very easily while other parts seem puzzling. In fact, very early in the history of the church Peter reminded his readers that some parts of Paul's epistles were difficult to understand: "So also our beloved brother Paul wrote to you according to the wisdom given him, speaking of this as he does in all his letters. There are some things in them *hard to understand,* which the ignorant and unstable twist to their own destruction, as they do the other scriptures" (2 Peter 3:15–16). We must admit therefore that not all parts of Scripture are able to be understood easily.

But it would be a mistake to think that most of Scripture or Scripture in general is difficult to understand. In fact, the Old Testament and New Testament frequently affirm that Scripture is written in such a way that its teachings are able to be understood by ordinary believers. Even in Peter's statement just quoted, the context is an appeal to the teachings of Paul's letter, which Peter's readers had read and understood (2 Peter 3:15). In fact, Peter assigns some moral blame to those who twist these passages "to their own destruction." And he does not say that there are things impossible to understand, but only difficult to understand.

### A. The Bible Frequently Affirms Its Own Clarity

The Bible's clarity and the responsibility of believers generally to read it and understand it are often emphasized. In a very familiar passage, Moses tells the people of Israel:

> And these words which I command you this day shall be upon your heart; and
> *you shall teach them diligently to your children,* and shall *talk of them* when you

sit in your house, and when you walk by the way, and when you lie down, and when you rise. (Deut. 6:6–7)

All the people of Israel were expected to be able to understand the words of Scripture well enough to be able to "teach them diligently" to their children. This teaching would not have consisted merely of rote memorization devoid of understanding, for the people of Israel were to *discuss* the words of Scripture during their activities of sitting in the house or walking or going to bed or getting up in the morning. God expected that *all* of his people would know and be able to talk about his Word, with proper application to ordinary situations in life. Similarly, Psalm 1 tells us that the "blessed man," whom all the righteous in Israel were to emulate, was one who meditated on God's law "day and night" (Ps. 1:2). This daily meditation assumes an ability to understand Scripture rightly on the part of those who meditate.

The character of Scripture is said to be such that even the "simple" can understand it rightly and be made wise by it. "The testimony of the LORD is sure, *making wise the simple*" (Ps. 19:7). Again we read, "The unfolding of your words gives light; *it imparts understanding to the simple*" (Ps. 119:130). Here the "simple" person (Heb. *petî*) is not merely one who lacks intellectual ability, but one who lacks sound judgment, who is prone to making mistakes, and who is easily led astray.[1] God's Word is so understandable, so clear, that even this kind of person is made wise by it. This should be a great encouragement to all believers: no believer should think himself or herself too foolish to read Scripture and understand it sufficiently to be made wise by it.

There is a similar emphasis in the New Testament. Jesus himself, in his teachings, his conversations, and his disputes, never responds to any questions with a hint of blaming the Old Testament Scriptures for being unclear. Even while speaking to first-century people who were removed from David by 1,000 years, from Moses by about 1,500 years, and from Abraham by about 2,000 years, Jesus still assumes that such people are able to read and rightly to understand the Old Testament Scriptures.

In a day when it is common for people to tell us how hard it is to interpret Scripture rightly, we would do well to remember that not once in the Gospels do we ever hear Jesus saying anything like this: "I see how your problem arose—the Scriptures are not very clear on that subject." Instead, whether he is speaking to scholars or untrained common people, his responses always assume that the blame for misunderstanding any teaching of Scripture is not to be placed on the Scriptures themselves, but on those who misunderstand or fail to accept what is written. Again and again he answers questions with statements like, "Have you not read . . ." (Matt. 12:3, 5; 19:4; 22:31), "Have you never read in the scriptures . . ." (Matt. 21:42), or even, "You are wrong because you know neither the Scriptures nor the power of God" (Matt. 22:29; cf. Matt. 9:13; 12:7; 15:3; 21:13; John 3:10, et al.).

Similarly, most of the New Testament epistles are written not to church leaders but to entire congregations. Paul writes, "To the church of God which is at Corinth" (1 Cor.

---

[1]Compare the use of this same word in Prov. 1:4; 7:7; 8:5; 9:6; 14:15, 18; 22:3; 27:12.

1:2), "To the churches of Galatia" (Gal. 1:2), "To all the saints in Christ Jesus who are at Philippi, with the bishops and deacons" (Phil. 1:1), and so forth. Paul *assumes* that his hearers will *understand* what he writes, and he encourages the sharing of his letters with other churches: "And when this letter has been read among you, have it read also in the church of the Laodiceans; and see that you read also the letter from Laodicea" (Col. 4:16; cf. John 20:30–31; 2 Cor. 1:13; Eph. 3:4; 1 Tim. 4:13; James 1:1, 22–25; 1 Peter 1:1; 2:2; 2 Peter 1:19; 1 John 5:13).[2]

Second Peter 1:20 may be urged against the view of the clarity of Scripture explained in this chapter. The verse says, "no prophecy of scripture is a matter of one's own interpretation," and someone may claim that this means that ordinary believers are unable to interpret Scripture rightly for themselves. It is unlikely, however, that this implication should be drawn from 2 Peter 1:20, for the verse is probably discussing the *origin* and not the interpretation of Scripture. Thus the NIV translates it, "no prophecy of Scripture *came about by* the prophet's own interpretation."[3] Furthermore, even if the verse were understood as speaking of interpreting Scripture, it would be saying that the interpretation of Scripture must be done within the fellowship of believers and not merely as a personal activity. It still would not be implying that authoritative interpreters are needed to ascertain the true meaning of Scripture, but simply that reading and understanding Scripture should not be carried out entirely in isolation from other Christians.

Lest we think that understanding the Bible was somehow easier for first-century Christians than for us, it is important to realize that in many instances the New Testament epistles were written to churches that had large proportions of Gentile Christians. They were relatively new Christians who had no previous background in any kind of Christian society, and who had little or no prior understanding of the history and culture of Israel. Nevertheless, the New Testament authors show no hesitancy in expecting even these Gentile Christians to be able to read a translation of the Old Testament in their own language and to understand it rightly (cf. Rom. 4:1–25; 15:4; 1 Cor. 10:1–11; 2 Tim. 3:16–17, et al.).

## B. The Moral and Spiritual Qualities Needed for Right Understanding

The New Testament writers frequently state that the ability to understand Scripture rightly is more a moral and spiritual than intellectual ability: "The unspiritual man does not receive the gifts [literally "things"] of the Spirit of God, for they are folly to him, and he is not able to understand them because they are spiritually discerned" (1 Cor. 2:14; cf. 1:18–3:4; 2 Cor. 3:14–16; 4:3–4, 6; Heb. 5:14; James 1:5–6; 2 Peter 3:5; cf. Mark

---

[2]Paul tells the Corinthians, "We write you nothing but what you can read and understand," and then he adds, "I hope you will understand fully, as you have understood in part" (2 Cor. 1:13–14). The addition to his first statement does not negate his affirmation of the clarity of what he has written to them, but does encourage the Corinthians to be diligent in listening carefully to Paul's words, in order that their partial understanding may be deepened and enriched. Indeed, the very expression of

such a hope shows that Paul assumes his writings are able to be understood (*elpizō*, "I hope," in the New Testament expresses a much more confident expectation of a future event than does the English word *hope*).

[3]This interpretation is well defended by Michael Green, *The Second Epistle of Peter and the Epistle of Jude,* TNTC (Grand Rapids: Eerdmans, 1987), pp. 100–102.

4:11–12; John 7:17; 8:43). Thus, although the New Testament authors affirm that the Bible *in itself* is written clearly, they also affirm that it will not be understood rightly by those who are unwilling to receive its teachings. Scripture is able to be understood by all unbelievers who will read it sincerely seeking salvation, and by all believers who will read it while seeking God's help in understanding it. This is because in both cases the Holy Spirit is at work overcoming the effects of sin, which otherwise will make the truth appear to be foolish (1 Cor. 2:14; 1:18–25; James 1:5–6, 22–25).

## C. Definition of the Clarity of Scripture

In order to summarize this biblical material, we can affirm that the Bible is written in such a way that all things necessary for our salvation and for our Christian life and growth are very clearly set forth in Scripture. Although theologians have sometimes defined the clarity of Scripture more narrowly (by saying, for example, only that Scripture is clear in teaching the way of salvation), the many texts cited above apply to many different aspects of biblical teaching and do not seem to support any such limitation on the areas to which Scripture can be said to speak clearly. It seems more faithful to those biblical texts to define the clarity[4] of Scripture as follows: *The clarity of Scripture means that the Bible is written in such a way that its teachings are able to be understood by all who will read it seeking God's help and being willing to follow it.* Once we have stated this, however, we must also recognize that many people, even God's people, do in fact misunderstand Scripture.

## D. Why Do People Misunderstand Scripture?

During Jesus' lifetime, his own disciples at times failed to understand the Old Testament and Jesus' own teachings (see Matt. 15:16; Mark 4:10–13; 6:52; 8:14–21; 9:32; Luke 18:34; John 8:27; 10:6). Although sometimes this was due to the fact that they simply needed to wait for further events in the history of redemption, and especially in the life of Christ himself (see John 12:16; 13:7; cf. John 2:22), there were also times when this was due to their own lack of faith or hardness of heart (Luke 24:25). Furthermore, there were times in the early church when Christians did not understand or agree on the teachings of the Old Testament or about the letters written by the apostles: note the process of growth in understanding concerning the implications of Gentile inclusion in the church (culminating in "much debate" [Acts 15:7] in the Jerusalem Council of Acts 15), or Peter's misunderstanding of this issue in Galatians 2:11–15, or the frequent doctrinal and ethical issues that had to be corrected by the New Testament epistles. In fact, throughout the history of the church, doctrinal disagreements have been many, and progress in resolving doctrinal differences has often been slow.

In order to help people to avoid making mistakes in interpreting Scripture, many Bible teachers have developed "principles of interpretation," or guidelines to encourage

---

[4]The old term for the clarity of Scripture was *perspicuity,* a term that simply means "clarity." That term itself is not very clear to people today, and I have not used it in this book.

growth in the skill of proper interpretation. The word *hermeneutics* (from the Greek word *hermēneuō*, "to interpret") is the more technical term for this field of study: *hermeneutics is the study of correct methods of interpretation* (especially interpretation of Scripture).

Another technical term often used in discussions of biblical interpretation is "exegesis," a term that refers more to the actual practice of interpreting Scripture, not to theories and principles about how it should be done: *exegesis is the process of interpreting a text of Scripture.* Consequently, when one studies principles of interpretation, that is "hermeneutics," but when one applies those principles and begins actually explaining a biblical text, he or she is doing "exegesis."

The existence of many disagreements about the meaning of Scripture throughout history reminds us that the doctrine of the clarity of Scripture does not imply or suggest that all believers will agree on all the teachings of Scripture. Nevertheless, it does tell us something very important—that the problem always lies not with Scripture but with ourselves. The situation is in fact similar to that of the authority of Scripture. Whereas we affirm that the words of Scripture have all the authority of God himself, we also realize that many people do not acknowledge that authority or submit themselves to it. Similarly, we affirm that all the teachings of Scripture are clear and able to be understood, but we also recognize that people often (through their own shortcomings) misunderstand what is clearly written in Scripture.

### E. Practical Encouragement From This Doctrine

The doctrine of the clarity of Scripture therefore has a very important, and ultimately very encouraging, practical implication. It tells us that where there are areas of doctrinal or ethical disagreement (for example, over baptism or predestination or church government), there are only two possible causes for these disagreements: (1) On the one hand, it may be that we are *seeking to make affirmations where Scripture itself is silent.* In such cases we should be more ready to admit that God has not given us the answer to our quest, and to allow for differences of viewpoint within the church. (This will often be the case with very practical questions, such as methods of evangelism or styles of Bible teaching or appropriate church size.) (2) On the other hand, it is possible that we have made *mistakes in our interpretation* of Scripture. This could have happened because the data we used to decide a question of interpretation were inaccurate or incomplete. Or it could be because there is some personal inadequacy on our part, whether it be, for example, personal pride, or greed, or lack of faith, or selfishness, or even failure to devote enough time to prayerfully reading and studying Scripture.

But in no case are we free to say that the teaching of the Bible on any subject is confusing or incapable of being understood correctly. In no case should we think that persistent disagreements on some subject through the history of the church mean that we will be unable to come to a correct conclusion on that subject ourselves. Rather, if a genuine concern about some such subject arises in our lives, we should sincerely ask God's help and then go to Scripture, searching it with all our ability, believing that God will enable us to understand rightly.

This truth should give great encouragement to all Christians to read their Bibles daily and with great eagerness. We should never assume, for example, that only those who know Greek and Hebrew, or only pastors or Bible scholars, are able to understand the Bible rightly — remember that the Old Testament was written in Hebrew and that many of the Christians to whom the New Testament letters were written had no knowledge of Hebrew at all: they had to read the Old Testament in a Greek translation. Yet the New Testament authors assume that these people can read it and understand it rightly even without scholarly ability in the original language. Christians must never give up to the scholarly "experts" the task of interpreting Scripture: they must keep doing it every day for themselves.[5]

Furthermore, even though we admit that there have been many doctrinal disagreements in the history of the church, we must not forget that there has been an amazing amount of doctrinal agreement on the most central truths of Scripture throughout the history of the church. Indeed, those who have had opportunities for fellowship with Christians in other parts of the world have discovered the remarkable fact that wherever we find a group of vital Christians, almost immediately a vast amount of agreement on all the central doctrines of the Christian faith becomes apparent. Why is this true, no matter what the society, or culture, or denominational affiliation? It is because they all have been reading and believing the same Bible, and its primary teachings have been clear.

## F. The Role of Scholars

Is there any role then for Bible scholars or for those with specialized knowledge of Hebrew (for the Old Testament) and Greek (for the New Testament)? Certainly there is a role for them in at least four areas:

1. They can *teach* Scripture clearly, communicating its content to others and thus fulfilling the office of "teacher" mentioned in the New Testament (1 Cor. 12:28; Eph. 4:11).

2. They can *explore* new areas of understanding the teachings of Scripture. This exploration will seldom (if ever) involve denial of the main teachings the church has held throughout its centuries, but it will often involve the application of Scripture to new areas of life, the answering of difficult questions that have been raised by both believers and unbelievers at each new period in history, and the continual activity of refining and making more precise the church's understanding of detailed points of interpretation of individual verses or matters of doctrine or ethics. Though the Bible may not seem large in comparison with the vast amount of literature in the world, it is a rich treasure-house of wisdom from God that surpasses in value all the other books that have ever been written. The process of relating its various teachings to one another, synthesizing them, and applying them to each new generation, is a greatly rewarding task that will never be

---

[5]I do not mean to suggest that the activity of interpreting Scripture should be an individualistic one: God will often use the writings of others or the personal advice of others to enable us to understand his Word rightly. The main point is that by whatever means, and primarily through the means of reading Scripture for themselves, Christians should expect that they will be enabled by God to understand the teachings of Scripture rightly.

completed in this age. Every scholar who deeply loves God's Word will soon realize that there is much more in Scripture than can be learned in any one lifetime!

3. They can *defend* the teachings of the Bible against attacks by other scholars or those with specialized technical training. The role of teaching God's Word also at times involves correcting false teachings. One must be able not only "to give instruction in sound doctrine" but also "to confute those who contradict it" (Titus 1:9; cf. 2 Tim. 2:25, "correcting his opponents with gentleness"; and Titus 2:7 – 8). Sometimes those who attack biblical teachings have specialized training and technical knowledge in historical, linguistic, or philosophical study, and they use that training to mount rather sophisticated attacks against the teaching of Scripture. In such cases, believers with similar specialized skills can use their training to understand and respond to such attacks. Such training is also very useful in responding to the false teachings of cults and sects. This is not to say that believers without specialized training are incapable of responding to false teaching (for most false teaching can be clearly refuted by a believer who prays and has a good knowledge of the English Bible), but rather that technical points in arguments can only be answered by those with skills in the technical areas appealed to.

4. They can *supplement* the study of Scripture for the benefit of the church. Bible scholars often have training that will enable them to relate the teachings of Scripture to the rich history of the church, and to make the interpretation of Scripture more precise and its meaning more vivid with a greater knowledge of the languages and cultures in which the Bible was written.

These four functions benefit the church as a whole, and all believers should be thankful for those who perform them. However, these functions do *not* include the right to decide for the church as a whole what is true and false doctrine or what is proper conduct in a difficult situation. If such a right were the preserve of formally trained Bible scholars, then they would become a governing elite in the church, and the ordinary functioning of the government of the church as described in the New Testament would cease. The process of decision-making for the church must be left to the officers of the church, whether they are scholars or not (and, in a congregational form of church government, not only to the officers but also to the people of the church as a whole).

## QUESTIONS FOR PERSONAL APPLICATION

1. If the doctrine of the clarity of Scripture is true, why does there seem to be so much disagreement among Christians about the teaching of the Bible? Observing the diversity of interpretations of Scripture, some conclude, "People can make the Bible say anything they want." How do you think Jesus would respond to this statement?

2. What would happen to the church if most believers gave up reading the Bible for themselves and only listened to Bible teachers or read books about the Bible? If you thought that only expert scholars could understand the Bible rightly, what would happen to your personal reading of Scripture? Has this already happened to some extent in your life or in the lives of those you know?

3. Do you think that there are right and wrong interpretations of most or all passages of Scripture? If you thought the Bible was generally unclear, how would your answer change? Will a conviction about the clarity of Scripture affect the care you use when studying a text of Scripture? Will it affect the way you approach Scripture when trying to gain a biblical answer to some difficult doctrinal or moral problem?

4. If even seminary professors disagree about some Bible teaching, can other Christians ever hope to come to a correct decision on that teaching? (Give reasons for your answer.) Do you think ordinary people among the Jews at the time of Jesus had a hard time deciding whether to believe Jesus or the scholarly experts who disagreed with him? Did Jesus expect them to be able to decide?

5. How can a pastor preach biblically based sermons each Sunday without giving the impression that only people with seminary training (like himself) are able to interpret Scripture rightly? Do you think it should ever be necessary, in a doctrinal or ethical controversy, for a Bible scholar to speak in a church and base his main arguments on special meanings of Greek or Hebrew words that the church members themselves are unable to evaluate or take issue with personally? Is there an appropriate way for a scholar to use such technical knowledge in popular writing or speaking?

6. Church leaders at the time of Martin Luther said they wanted to keep the Bible in Latin to prevent the common people from reading it and then misinterpreting it. Evaluate this argument. Why do you think Martin Luther was so anxious to translate the Bible into German? Why do you think church leaders in previous centuries have persecuted and even killed men—like William Tyndale in England—who were translating the Bible into the language of the people? Why is the task of Bible translation into other languages so important a part of the work of missions?

7. Does the doctrine of the clarity of Scripture mean that the New Testament can be fully understood by people who do not have access to an Old Testament?

## SPECIAL TERMS

clarity of Scripture

exegesis

hermeneutics

perspicuity

## BIBLIOGRAPHY

In this section I have listed several works on developing greater skill in biblical interpretation, including three helpful works by nonevangelical authors (one by Barr and two by Hirsch).

Barr, James. *The Semantics of Biblical Language.* London: Oxford University Press, 1961.

Berkhof, Louis. *Principles of Biblical Interpretation.* Grand Rapids: Baker, 1950.

Carson, D. A. *Exegetical Fallacies.* Grand Rapids: Baker, 1984.

Dockery, David S. *Biblical Interpretation Then and Now: Contemporary Hermeneutics in the Light of the Early Church.* Grand Rapids: Baker, 1992.

Fee, Gordon D., and Douglas Stuart. *How to Read the Bible for All Its Worth.* Grand Rapids: Zondervan, 1982.

Hirsch, E. D., Jr. *The Aims of Interpretation.* Chicago: University of Chicago Press, 1976.

_____. *Validity in Interpretation.* New Haven and London: Yale University Press, 1967.

Hubbard, Robert L., William W. Klein, and Craig L. Blomberg. *Introduction to Biblical Interpretation.* Waco, Tex.: Word Books, 1993.

Inch, Morris A., and C. Hassell Bullock, eds. *The Literature and Meaning of Scripture.* Grand Rapids: Baker, 1981.

Kaiser, Walter C., Jr. *Toward an Exegetical Theology.* Grand Rapids: Baker, 1982.

Marshall, I. Howard, ed. *New Testament Interpretation: Essays on Principles and Methods.* Grand Rapids: Eerdmans, 1977.

McCown, Wayne, and James Earl Massey, eds. *Interpreting God's Word for Today: An Inquiry Into Hermeneutics From a Biblical Theological Perspective. Wesleyan Theological Perspectives,* vol. 2. Anderson, Ind.: Warner Press, 1982.

McKnight, Scot, ed. *Introducing New Testament Interpretation.* Grand Rapids: Baker, 1990.

_____. *Interpreting the Synoptic Gospels.* Grand Rapids: Baker, 1988.

Mickelsen, A. Berkeley. *Interpreting the Bible.* Grand Rapids: Eerdmans, 1963.

Osborne, Grant R. *The Hermeneutical Spiral: A Comprehensive Introduction to Biblical Interpretation.* Downers Grove, Ill.: InterVarsity Press, 1992.

Packer, J. I. "Infallible Scripture and the Role of Hermeneutics." In *Scripture and Truth.* Ed. by D. A. Carson and John Woodbridge. Grand Rapids: Zondervan, 1983, pp. 325–56.

_____. "Scripture." In *NDT,* pp. 627–31.

Ramm, Bernard. *Protestant Biblical Interpretation.* 3d ed. Grand Rapids: Baker, 1970.

Schultz, Samuel J., and Morris A. Inch, eds. *Interpreting the Word of God. Festschrift in Honor of Steven Barabas.* Chicago: Moody, 1976.

Silva, Moises. *Biblical Words and Their Meanings.* Grand Rapids: Zondervan, 1983.

_____. *Has the Church Misread the Bible? The History of Interpretation in the Light of Contemporary Issues.* Grand Rapids: Zondervan, 1987.

Sire, James. *Scripture Twisting: Twenty Ways the Cults Misread the Bible.* Downers Grove, Ill.: InterVarsity Press, 1980.

Sproul, R. C. *Knowing Scripture.* Downers Grove, Ill.: InterVarsity Press, 1977.

Thiselton, Anthony C. *New Horizons in Hermeneutics: The Theory and Practice of Transforming Biblical Reading.* Grand Rapids: Zondervan, 1992.

_____. *The Two Horizons: New Testament Hermeneutics and Philosophical Description.* Grand Rapids: Eerdmans, 1980.

## SCRIPTURE MEMORY PASSAGE

**Deuteronomy 6:6–7:** *And these words which I command you this day shall be upon your heart; and you shall teach them diligently to your children, and shall talk of them when you sit in your house, and when you walk by the way, and when you lie down, and when you rise.*

## HYMN

### "Jehovah's Perfect Law"

This section of Psalm 19 set to music reminds us of many excellent qualities of Scripture, among them the fact that it is written clearly: "The testimony of the LORD is sure, making wise the simple" (v. 7).

(Use the tune of "We Come, O Christ, to You.")

> Jehovah's perfect law restores the soul again;
> His testimony sure gives wisdom unto men;
> The precepts of the LORD are right,
> And fill the heart with great delight.
>
> The LORD's commands are pure; they light and joy restore;
> Jehovah's fear is clean, enduring evermore;
> His statutes, let the world confess,
> Are wholly truth and righteousness.
>
> They are to be desired above the finest gold;
> Than honey from the comb more sweetness far they hold;
> With warnings they your servant guard,
> In keeping them is great reward.
>
> His errors who can know? Cleanse me from hidden stain;
> Keep me from willful sins, nor let them o'er me reign;
> And then I upright shall appear
> And be from great transgressions clear.
>
> Whene'er you search my life, may all my thoughts within
> And all the words I speak your full approval win.
> O Lord, you are a rock to me,
> And my Redeemer you shall be.

FROM: *THE PSALTER*, 1912 (TAKEN FROM PS. 19:7–14)

# Chapter 7

# THE FOUR CHARACTERISTICS OF SCRIPTURE: (3) NECESSITY

*For what purposes are the Bible necessary?*
*How much can people know about God*
*without the Bible?*

Do we need to have a Bible or to have someone tell us what the Bible says in order to know that God exists? Or that we are sinners needing to be saved? Or to know how to find salvation? Or to know God's will for our lives? These are the kinds of questions which an investigation of the necessity of Scripture is intended to answer.

## EXPLANATION AND SCRIPTURAL BASIS

The necessity of Scripture may be defined as follows: *The necessity of Scripture means that the Bible is necessary for knowing the gospel, for maintaining spiritual life, and for knowing God's will, but is not necessary for knowing that God exists or for knowing something about God's character and moral laws.*

That definition may now be explained in its various parts.[1]

### A. The Bible Is Necessary for Knowledge of the Gospel

In Romans 10:13–17 Paul says:

For, "everyone who calls upon the name of the Lord will be saved." But how are men to call upon him in whom they have not believed? And *how are they to believe in him of whom they have never heard?* And how are they to hear without

---

[1]As the subsequent sections indicate, when this definition says that the Bible is necessary for certain things, I do not mean to imply that an actual printed copy of the Bible is necessary for every person, because sometimes people hear the Bible read aloud or hear others tell them some of the contents of the Bible. But even these oral communications of the contents of the Bible are based on the existence of written copies of the Bible to which other people have access.

a preacher? . . . So *faith comes from what is heard,* and what is heard comes by the preaching of Christ.

This statement indicates the following line of reasoning: (1) It first assumes that one must call upon the name of the Lord to be saved. (In Pauline usage generally as well as in this specific context [see v. 9], "the Lord" refers to the Lord Jesus Christ.) (2) People can only call upon the name of Christ if they believe in him (that is, that he is a Savior worthy of calling upon and one who will answer those who call). (3) People cannot believe in Christ unless they have heard of him. (4) They cannot hear of Christ unless there is someone to tell them about Christ (a "preacher"). (5) The conclusion is that saving faith comes by hearing (that is, by hearing the gospel message), and this hearing of the gospel message comes about through the preaching of Christ. The implication seems to be that without hearing the preaching of the gospel of Christ, no one can be saved.[2]

This passage is one of several that show that eternal salvation comes only through belief in Jesus Christ and no other way. Speaking of Christ, John 3:18 says, "He who believes in him is not condemned; *he who does not believe is condemned already,* because he has not believed in the name of the only Son of God." Similarly, in John 14:6 Jesus says, "I am the way, and the truth, and the life; *no one comes to the Father, but by me.*"

Peter, on trial before the Sanhedrin, says, "*there is salvation in no one else,* for there is *no other name* under heaven given among men by which we must be saved" (Acts 4:12). Of course, the exclusiveness of salvation through Christ is because Jesus is the only one who ever died for our sins or whoever could have done so. Paul says, "For there is one God, and *there is one mediator between God and men, the man Christ Jesus, who gave himself as a ransom for all . . .*" (1 Tim. 2:5–6). There is no other way to be reconciled to God than through Christ, for there is no other way of dealing with the guilt of our sin before a holy God.

But if people can be saved only through faith in Christ, someone might ask how believers under the old covenant could have been saved. The answer must be that those who were saved under the old covenant were also saved through trusting in Christ, even though their faith was a forward-looking faith based on God's word of promise that a Messiah or a Redeemer would come. Speaking of Old Testament believers such as Abel, Enoch, Noah, Abraham, and Sarah, the author of Hebrews says, "*These all died in faith,* not having received what was promised, but *having seen it and greeted it from afar . . .*" (Heb. 11:13). The same chapter goes on to say that Moses "considered abuse suffered *for the Christ* (or the Messiah) greater wealth than the treasures of Egypt, for he looked to the reward" (Heb. 11:26). And Jesus can say of Abraham, "Your father Abraham rejoiced that he was to see my day; *he saw it* and was glad" (John 8:56). This again apparently refers to Abraham's joy in looking forward to the day of the promised Messiah. Thus,

---

[2]Someone might object that the following verse, Rom. 10:18, in its quotation of Ps. 19:4, "Their voice has gone out to all the earth, and their words to the ends of the world," implies that all people everywhere have already heard the gospel message or the message of Christ. But in the context of Psalm 19, verse 4 only speaks of the fact that the natural creation, especially the heavens above, proclaim God's glory and the greatness of his creative activity. There is no thought here of the proclamation of salvation through Christ. The idea that all people everywhere have heard the gospel of Christ through natural revelation would also be contrary to Paul's missionary activities.

even Old Testament believers had saving faith in Christ, to whom they looked forward, not with exact knowledge of the historical details of Christ's life, but with great faith in the absolute reliability of God's word of promise.

The Bible is necessary for salvation, then, in this sense: one must either read the gospel message in the Bible for oneself, or hear it from another person. Even those believers who came to salvation in the old covenant did so by trusting in the words of God that promised a Savior to come.

In fact, these repeated instances of people trusting in God's *words* of promise, together with the verses above that affirm the necessity of hearing about and believing in Christ, seem to indicate that sinful people need more on which to rest their faith than just an intuitive guess that God might provide a means of salvation. It seems that the only foundation firm enough to rest one's faith on is the *word* of God itself (whether spoken or written). This in the earliest times came in very brief form, but from the very beginning we have evidence of *words* of God promising a salvation yet to come, words that were trusted by those people whom God called to himself.

For example, even in the lifetime of Adam and Eve there are some words of God that point toward a future salvation: in Genesis 3:15 the curse on the serpent includes a promise that the seed of the woman (one of her descendants) would bruise the head of the serpent but would himself be hurt in the process—a promise ultimately fulfilled in Christ. The fact that the first two children of Adam and Eve, Cain and Abel, offered sacrifices to the LORD (Gen. 4:3–4) indicates their consciousness of a need to make some kind of payment for the guilt of their sin, and of God's promise of acceptance of sacrifices offered in the right way. Genesis 4:7, "If you do well, will you not be accepted?" indicates again in the very briefest form a word from God that offered the provision of some kind of salvation through trusting in the promise of God offered in that word. As the history of the Old Testament progressed, God's words of promise became more and more specific, and the forward-looking faith of God's people accordingly became more and more definite. Yet it seems always to have been a faith resting specifically on the *words* of God himself.

Thus, although it will be argued below that people can know that God *exists* and can know something of his *laws* apart from Scripture, it seems that there is no possibility of coming to *saving faith* apart from specific knowledge of God's words of promise.

## B. The Bible Is Necessary for Maintaining Spiritual Life

Jesus says in Matthew 4:4 (quoting Deut. 8:3), "Man shall not live on bread alone, but on every word that proceeds out of the mouth of God" (NASB). Here Jesus indicates that our spiritual life is maintained by daily nourishment with the Word of God, just as our physical lives are maintained by daily nourishment with physical food. To neglect regular reading of God's Word is as detrimental to the health of our souls as the neglect of physical food is detrimental to the health of our bodies.

Similarly, Moses tells the people of Israel of the importance of God's words for their lives: "For it is no trifle for you, but *it is your life,* and thereby you shall live long in the land which you are going over the Jordan to possess" (Deut. 32:47). And Peter encourages the Christians to whom he writes, "Like newborn babes, long for the pure spiritual milk, that by it you may grow up to salvation" (1 Peter 2:2). The "pure spiritual milk" in this context must refer to the Word of God about which Peter has been speaking (see 1 Peter 1:23–25). The Bible, then, is necessary for maintaining spiritual life and for growth in the Christian life.

## C. The Bible Is Necessary for Certain Knowledge of God's Will

It will be argued below that all people ever born have *some* knowledge of God's will through their consciences. But this knowledge is often indistinct and cannot give certainty. In fact, if there were *no* written Word of God, we *could not* gain certainty about God's will through other means such as conscience, advice from others, an internal witness of the Holy Spirit, changed circumstances, and the use of sanctified reasoning and common sense. These all might give an approximation of God's will in more or less reliable ways, but from these means alone no certainty about God's will could ever be attained, at least in a fallen world where sin distorts our perception of right and wrong, brings faulty reasoning into our thinking processes, and causes us to suppress from time to time the testimony of our consciences (cf. Jer. 17:9; Rom. 2:14–15; 1 Cor. 8:10; Heb. 5:14; 10:22; also 1 Tim. 4:2; Titus 1:15).

In the Bible, however, we have clear and definite statements about God's will. God has not revealed all things to us, but he has revealed enough for us to know his will: "The secret things belong to the Lord our God; but *the things that are revealed belong to us and to our children for ever, that we may do all the words of this law*" (Deut. 29:29). As it was in the time of Moses, so it is now with us: God has revealed his words to us that we might obey his laws and thereby do his will. To be "blameless" in God's sight is to "walk in the law of the Lord" (Ps. 119:1). The "blessed" man is one who does not follow the will of wicked people (Ps. 1:1), but delights "*in the law of the Lord,*" and meditates on God's law "day and night" (Ps. 1:2). To love God (and thereby to act in a way that is pleasing to him) is to "keep his commandments" (1 John 5:3). If we are to have a certain knowledge of God's will, then, we must attain it through the study of Scripture.

In fact, in one sense it can be argued that the Bible is necessary for certain knowledge about anything. A philosopher might argue as follows: The fact that we do not know everything requires us to be uncertain about everything we do claim to know. This is because some fact unknown to us may yet turn out to prove that what we thought to be true was actually false. For example, we think we know our date of birth, our name, our age, and so forth. But we must admit that it is possible that some day we could find that our parents had given us false information and our "certain" knowledge would then turn out to be incorrect. Regarding events that we personally have experienced, we all realize how it is possible for us to "remember" words or events incorrectly and find ourselves later corrected by more accurate information. We can usually be more certain about the events of our present experience, so long as it remains present (but even that, someone might argue, could be a dream, and we will only discover this fact when we wake up!). At any rate, it is difficult to answer the philosopher's question: If we do not know *all* the facts in the universe, past, present, and future, how can we ever attain *certainty* that we have correct information about any one fact?

Ultimately, there are only two possible solutions to this problem: (1) We must learn all the facts of the universe in order to be sure that no subsequently discovered fact will prove our present ideas to be false; or (2) someone who *does* know all the facts in the universe, and who never lies, could tell us some true facts that we can then be sure will never be contradicted.

This second solution is in fact what we have when we have God's words in Scripture. God knows all facts that ever have been or ever will be. And this God who is omniscient (all-knowing) has absolutely certain knowledge: there can never be any fact that he does not already know; thus, there can never be any fact that would prove that something God thinks is actually false. Now it is from this infinite storehouse of certain knowledge that God, who never lies, has spoken to us in Scripture, in which he has told us many true things about himself, about ourselves, and about the universe that he has made. No fact can ever turn up to contradict the truth spoken by this one who is omniscient.

Thus, it is appropriate for us to be *more certain* about the truths we read in Scripture than about any other knowledge we have. If we are to talk about degrees of certainty of knowledge we have, then the knowledge we attain from Scripture would have the highest degree of certainty: if the word "certain" can be applied to any kind of human knowledge, it can be applied to this knowledge.[3]

This concept of the certainty of knowledge that we attain from Scripture then gives us a reasonable basis for affirming the correctness of much of the other knowledge that we have. We read Scripture and find that its view of the world around us, of human nature, and of ourselves corresponds closely to the information we have gained from our own sense-experiences of the world around us. Thus we are encouraged to trust our sense-experiences of the world around us: our observations correspond with the absolute truth of Scripture; therefore, our observations are also true and, by and large, reliable. Such confidence in the general reliability of observations made with our eyes and ears is further confirmed by the fact that it is God who has made these faculties and who in Scripture frequently encourages us to use them (compare also Prov. 20:12: "The hearing ear and the seeing eye, the LORD has made them both").

In this way the Christian who takes the Bible as God's Word escapes from philosophical skepticism about the possibility of attaining certain knowledge with our finite minds.

---

[3]This statement assumes that we have become convinced that Scripture is indeed the very words of God, and that we have understood at least some portions of Scripture correctly. Yet at this point the doctrine of the clarity of Scripture discussed in the previous chapter assures us that we will be able to understand the teachings of Scripture correctly, and the overwhelming testimony of Scripture to its own divine authorship (discussed in the chapters above concerning different forms of the Word of God and concerning the authority of Scripture), made persuasive to us by the work of the Holy Spirit, convinces us of the divine authorship of Scripture. In this sense the argument becomes not so much circular as something like a spiral where each section of the doctrine of Scripture reinforces the other and deepens our persuasion of the truthfulness of other sections of the doctrine of Scripture. By this process, our persuasion that Scripture is God's Word, that it is truth, that it is clear, and that knowledge which we attain from it is certain, becomes stronger and stronger the more we study and reflect on it.

We can of course speak of degrees of certainty that we might have concerning the fact that the Bible is God's Word, and degrees of certainty that our interpretation of any one teaching in Scripture is correct. Then from the standpoint of individual personal experience, we could say that our certainty of the correctness of knowledge that we have from Scripture becomes greater in proportion to our certainty about the God-breathed character and clarity of Scripture.

Yet from a theological standpoint, if we begin with an agreement that Scripture is God-breathed and that we do understand its teachings (at least its major teachings) correctly, then it is appropriate to say that the knowledge we attain from Scripture is more certain than any other knowledge we have.

In this sense, then, it is correct to say that for people who are not omniscient, the Bible is necessary for certain knowledge about anything.

This fact is important for the following discussion, where we affirm that unbelievers *can* know something about God from the general revelation that is seen in the world around them. Although this is true, we must recognize that in a fallen world knowledge gained by observation of the world is always imperfect and always liable to error or misinterpretation. Therefore the knowledge of God and creation gained from Scripture must be used to interpret correctly the creation around us. Using the theological terms that we will define below, we can say that we need special revelation to interpret general revelation rightly.[4]

## D. But the Bible Is Not Necessary for Knowing That God Exists

What about people who do not read the Bible? Can they obtain any knowledge of God? Can they know anything about his laws? Yes, without the Bible some knowledge of God is possible, even if it is not absolutely certain knowledge.

People can obtain a knowledge *that God exists,* and a knowledge of *some of his attributes,* simply from observation of themselves and the world around them. David says, *"The heavens are telling the glory of God; and the firmament proclaims his handiwork"* (Ps. 19:1). To look at the sky is to see evidence of the infinite power, wisdom, and even beauty of God; it is to observe a majestic witness to the glory of God. Similarly, Barnabas and Paul tell the Greek inhabitants of Lystra about the living God who made the heavens and the earth: "In past generations he allowed all the nations to walk in their own ways; yet *he did not leave himself without witness,* for he did good and gave you from heaven rains and fruitful seasons, satisfying your hearts with food and gladness" (Acts 14:16 – 17). Rains and fruitful seasons, food produced from the earth, and gladness in people's hearts, all bear witness to the fact that their Creator is a God of mercy, of love, and even of joy. These evidences of God are all around us in creation to be seen by those who are willing to see them.

Even those who by their wickedness suppress the truth cannot avoid the evidences of God's existence and nature in the created order:

> For *what can be known about God is plain to them,* because God has shown it to them. Ever since the creation of the world *his invisible nature,* namely, his eternal power and deity, *has been clearly perceived in the things that have been made.* So they are without excuse; for although *they knew God* they did not honor him as God or give thanks to him, but they became futile in their thinking and their senseless minds were darkened. (Rom. 1:19 – 21)

Here Paul says not only that creation gives evidence of God's existence and character, but also that even wicked men recognize that evidence. What can be known about God is "plain to them" and in fact "they knew God" (apparently, they knew who he was), but "they did not honor him as God or give thanks to him." This passage allows us to say that all persons, even the most wicked, have some internal knowledge or perception that

---

[4]See section E for definitions of general revelation and special revelation.

God exists and that he is a powerful Creator. This knowledge is seen "in the things that have been made," a phrase that refers to all creation. Yet it is probably in seeing mankind created in the image of God—that is, in seeing both themselves and other people—that even wicked persons see the greatest evidence of God's existence and nature.[5]

Thus, even without the Bible, all persons who have ever lived have had evidence in creation that God exists, that he is the Creator and they are creatures, and have also had some evidence of his character. As a result, they themselves have known something about God from this evidence (even though this is never said to be a knowledge that is able to bring them to salvation).

### E. Furthermore, the Bible Is Not Necessary for Knowing Something About God's Character and Moral Laws

Paul goes on in Romans 1 to show that even unbelievers who have no written record of God's laws still have in their consciences some understanding of God's moral demands. Speaking of a long list of sins ("envy, murder, strife, deceit . . ."), Paul says of wicked people who practice them, "Though *they know God's decree that those who do such things deserve to die*, they not only do them but approve those who practice them" (Rom. 1:32). Wicked people know that their sin is wrong, at least in large measure.

Paul then talks about the activity of conscience in Gentiles who do not have the written law:

> When Gentiles who have not the law do by nature what the law requires, they are a law to themselves, even though they do not have the law. They show that *what the law requires is written on their hearts,* while their conscience also bears witness and their conflicting thoughts accuse or perhaps excuse them. . . . (Rom. 2:14–15)

The consciences of unbelievers bear witness to God's moral standards, but at times this evidence of God's law on the hearts of unbelievers is distorted or suppressed.[6] Sometimes their thoughts "accuse" them and sometimes their thoughts "excuse" them, Paul says. The knowledge of God's laws derived from such sources is never perfect, but it is enough to give an awareness of God's moral demands to all mankind. (And it is on this basis that Paul argues that all humanity is held guilty before God for sin, even those who do not have the written laws of God in Scripture.)

The knowledge of God's existence, character, and moral law, which comes through creation to all humanity, is often called "*general revelation*" (because it comes to all

---

[5]The Swiss theologian Karl Barth (1886–1968) denied that natural man can know anything of God through the general revelation found in nature, but insisted that knowledge of God can only come through a knowledge of God's grace in Christ. His radical rejection of natural revelation has not gained wide acceptance; it rests upon the unlikely view that Rom. 1:21 refers to a knowledge of God in theory but not in fact.

[6]The consciences of unbelievers will be suppressed or hardened in various areas of morality, depending on cultural influences and personal circumstances. A cannibalistic society, for example, will have many members whose consciences are hardened and insensitive with regard to the evil of murder, while modern American society, for example, exhibits very little sensitivity of conscience with regard to the evil of falsehood in speech, or disrespect for parental authority, or sexual immorality. Moreover, individuals who repeatedly commit a certain sin will often find the pangs of conscience diminishing after time: a thief may feel very guilty after his first or second robbery but feel little guilt after his twentieth. The witness of conscience is still there in each case, but it is suppressed through repeated wickedness.

people generally).[7] General revelation comes through observing nature, through seeing God's directing influence in history, and through an inner sense of God's existence and his laws that he has placed inside every person. General revelation is distinct from *"special revelation,"* which refers to God's words addressed to specific people, such as the words of the Bible, the words of the Old Testament prophets and New Testament apostles, and the words of God spoken in personal address, such as at Mount Sinai or at the baptism of Jesus.[8]

Special revelation includes all the words of Scripture but is not limited to the words of Scripture, for it also includes, for example, many words of Jesus that were not recorded in Scripture, and probably there were many words spoken by Old Testament prophets and New Testament apostles that were not recorded in Scripture either.

The fact that all people know something of God's moral laws is a great blessing for society, for unless they did there would be no societal restraint on the evil that people would do and no restraint from their consciences. Because there is some common knowledge of right and wrong, Christians can often find much consensus with non-Christians in matters of civil law, community standards, basic ethics for business and professional activity, and acceptable patterns of conduct in ordinary life. Moreover, we can appeal to the sense of rightness within people's hearts (Rom. 2:14) when attempting to enact better laws or overturn bad laws, or to right some other injustices in society around us. The knowledge of God's existence and character also provides a basis of information that enables the gospel to make sense to a non-Christian's heart and mind: unbelievers know that God exists and that they have broken his standards, so the news that Christ died to pay for their sins should truly come as *good news* to them.

However, it must be emphasized that Scripture nowhere indicates that people can know the gospel, or know the way of salvation, through such general revelation. They may know that God exists, that he is their Creator, that they owe him obedience, and that they have sinned against him. The existence of systems of sacrifice in primitive religions throughout history attests to the fact that these things can be clearly known by people apart from the Bible. The repeated occurrences of the "rain and fruitful seasons" mentioned in Acts 14:17 may even lead some people to reason that God is not only holy and righteous but also loving and forgiving. But how the *holiness and justice* of God can ever be reconciled with his *willingness to forgive sins* is a mystery that has never been solved by any religion apart from the Bible. Nor does the Bible give us any hope that it ever can be discovered apart from specific revelation from God. It is the great wonder of our redemption that God himself has provided the way of salvation by sending his own Son, who is both God and man, to be our representative and bear the penalty for our sins, thus combining the justice and love of God in one infinitely wise and amazingly gracious act. This fact, which seems commonplace to the Christian ear, should not lose its wonder for us: it could never have been conceived by man alone apart from God's special, verbal revelation.

---

[7]For an extensive discussion of the history of the doctrine of general revelation and its basis in Scripture, see Demarest, *General Revelation;* see also the excellent treatment of this doctrine in Gordon R. Lewis and Bruce A. Demarest, *Integrative Theology* (Grand Rapids: Zondervan, 1987). 1:59–91.

[8]See chapter 2, pp. 35–37, for a discussion of God's words of personal address, God's words spoken through the lips of human beings, and God's words in Scripture, all of which fall in the category of special revelation.

Furthermore, even if an adherent of a primitive religion could think that God somehow *must have* himself paid the penalty for our sins, such a thought would only be an extraordinary speculation. It could never be held with enough certainty to be the ground on which to rest saving faith unless God himself confirmed such speculation with his own words, namely, the words of the gospel proclaiming either that this indeed was going to happen (if the revelation came in the time before Christ) or that it indeed has happened (if the revelation came in the time after Christ). The Bible never views human speculation apart from the Word of God as a sufficient basis on which *to rest saving faith:* such saving faith, according to Scripture, is always confidence or trust in God that rests on the truthfulness of God's own words.[9]

## QUESTIONS FOR PERSONAL APPLICATION

1. When you are witnessing to an unbeliever, what is the one thing above all others that you should want him or her to read? Do you know of anyone who ever became a Christian without either reading the Bible or hearing someone tell him or her what the Bible said? What then is the primary task of an evangelistic missionary? How should the necessity of Scripture affect our missionary orientation?

2. Do you nourish your soul on the spiritual food of the Word as carefully and diligently as you nourish your body on physical food? What makes us so spiritually insensitive that we feel physical hunger much more acutely than spiritual hunger? What is the remedy?

3. When we are actively seeking to know God's will, where should we spend most of our time and effort? In practice, where do you spend most of your time and effort when seeking to find God's will? Do God's principles in Scripture and the apparent guidance we receive from feelings, conscience, advice, circumstances, human reasoning, or society ever seem to conflict? How should we seek to resolve the conflict?

4. Is it a hopeless task to work for civil legislation based on standards that accord with God's moral principles in Scripture? Why is there good reason to hope that we will finally be able to persuade a great majority of our society to adopt laws consistent with scriptural norms? What would hinder this effort?

## SPECIAL TERMS

| | |
|---|---|
| general revelation | necessity of Scripture |
| natural revelation | special revelation |

## BIBLIOGRAPHY

Berkouwer, G. C. *General Revelation*. (No translator named.) Grand Rapids: Eerdmans, 1955.

---

[9]In the New Testament, we should also note that it is specifically the Word of God that is said to be the agent that God uses in giving people spiritual life (James 1:18; 1 Peter 1:23).

Demarest, Bruce A. *General Revelation.* Grand Rapids: Zondervan, 1982.

_____. "Revelation, General." In *EDT*, pp. 944–45.

Henry, Carl F. H. "Revelation, Special." In *EDT*, pp. 945–48.

Kuyper, Abraham. *Principles of Sacred Theology.* Trans. by J. H. de Vries. Grand Rapids: Eerdmans, 1968, pp. 341–405 (originally published as *Encyclopedia of Sacred Theology* in 1898).

Packer, J. I. "Scripture." In *NDT*, pp. 627–31.

Van Til, Cornelius. *Common Grace and the Gospel.* Nutley, N.J.: Presbyterian and Reformed, 1973.

_____. *In Defense of the Faith,* vol. 1: *The Doctrine of Scripture.* Ripon, Calif.: den Dulk Christian Foundation, 1967, pp. 1–15.

_____. *In Defense of the Faith,* vol. 5: *An Introduction to Systematic Theology.* Phillipsburg, N.J.: Presbyterian and Reformed, 1976, pp. 62–109.

## SCRIPTURE MEMORY PASSAGE

**Matthew 4:4:** *But he answered, "It is written, 'Man shall not live by bread alone, but by every word that proceeds from the mouth of God.'"*

## HYMN

### "Teach Me, O Lord, Your Way of Truth"
(Use the familiar tune of "Jesus Shall Reign.")

Teach me, O Lord, your way of truth,
 And from it I will not depart;
That I may steadfastly obey,
 Give me an understanding heart.

In your commandments make me walk,
 For in your law my joy shall be;
Give me a heart that loves your will,
 From discontent and envy free.

Turn now my eyes from vanity,
 And cause me in your ways to tread;
O let your servant prove your Word
 and thus to godly fear be led.

Turn away my reproach and fear;
 Your righteous judgments I confess;
To know your precepts I desire;
 Revive me in your righteousness.

FROM: *THE PSALTER,* 1912 (TAKEN FROM PS. 119:33–40)

An alternative hymn for this chapter is a modern Scripture song, "Seek Ye First the Kingdom of God." The second verse of this song ("Man shall not live on bread alone. . .") is a quotation of Matthew 4:4 and expresses the necessity of Scripture for maintaining our spiritual life: we live on every word that proceeds from the mouth of God. The other verses of the song do not speak directly of the doctrine of the necessity of Scripture but do contain the words of gospel invitation (vv. 1, 4, 5). All verses in the song are direct quotations of Scripture, and, as such, will be spiritually nourishing for us to sing and meditate on.

# Chapter 8

# THE FOUR CHARACTERISTICS OF SCRIPTURE: (4) SUFFICIENCY

## *Is the Bible enough for knowing what God wants us to think or do?*

## EXPLANATION AND SCRIPTURAL BASIS

Are we to look for other words from God in addition to those we have in Scripture? The doctrine of the sufficiency of Scripture addresses this question.

### A. Definiton of the Sufficiency of Scripture

We can define the sufficiency of Scripture as follows: *The sufficiency of Scripture means that Scripture contained all the words of God he intended his people to have at each stage of redemptive history, and that it now contains all the words of God we need for salvation, for trusting him perfectly, and for obeying him perfectly.*

This definition emphasizes that it is in Scripture alone that we are to search for God's words to us. It also reminds us that God considers what he has told us in the Bible to be enough for us, and that we should rejoice in the great revelation that he has given us and be content with it.

Significant scriptural support and explanation of this doctrine is found in Paul's words to Timothy, "from childhood you have been acquainted with the sacred writings which are *able to instruct you for salvation* through faith in Christ Jesus" (2 Tim. 3:15). The context shows that "sacred writings" here means the written words of Scripture (2 Tim. 3:16). This is an indication that the words of God which we have in Scripture are all the words of God we need in order to be saved: these words are able to make us wise "for salvation." This is confirmed by other passages that talk about the words of Scripture as the means God uses to bring us to salvation (James 1:18; 1 Peter 1:23).

Other passages indicate that the Bible is sufficient to equip us for living the Christian life. Once again Paul writes to Timothy, "All scripture is inspired by God and profitable for teaching, for reproof, for correction, and for training in righteousness, *that the man of God may be complete, equipped for every good work*" (2 Tim. 3:16–17).

Here Paul indicates that one purpose for which God caused Scripture to be written is to train us that we might be "equipped for every good work." If there is any "good work" that God wants a Christian to do, this passage indicates that God has made provision in his Word for training the Christian in it. Thus, there is no "good work" that God wants us to do other than those that are taught somewhere in Scripture: it can equip us for *every* good work.

A similar teaching is found in Psalm 119: "Blessed are those whose way is *blameless* who *walk in the law of the Lord!*" (v. 1). This verse shows an equivalence between being "blameless" and "walking in the law of the Lord": those who are blameless are those who walk in the law of the Lord. Here again is an indication that all that God requires of us is recorded in his written Word: simply to do all that the Bible commands us is to be blameless in God's sight.

To be morally perfect in God's sight, then, what must we do in addition to what God commands us in Scripture? Nothing! Nothing at all! If we simply keep the words of Scripture we will be "blameless" and we will be doing "every good work" that God expects of us.

## B. We Can Find All That God Has Said on Particular Topics, and We Can Find Answers to Our Questions

Of course, we realize that we will never perfectly obey all of Scripture in this life (see James 3:2; 1 John 1:8–10). Thus, it may not at first seem very significant to say that all we have to do is what God commands us in the Bible, since we will never be able to obey it all in this life anyway. But the truth of the sufficiency of Scripture is of great significance for our Christian lives, for it enables us to *focus* our search for God's words to us on the Bible alone and saves us from the endless task of searching through all the writings of Christians throughout history, or through all the teachings of the church, or through all the subjective feelings and impressions that come to our minds from day to day,[1] in order to find what God requires of us. In a very practical sense, it means that we are able to come to clear conclusions on many teachings of Scripture. For example, though it

---

[1]This is not meant to imply that subjective impressions of God's will are useless or that they should be ignored. That would suggest almost a deistic view of God's (non-)involvement in the lives of his children and a rather mechanical, impersonal view of guidance. God can and indeed does use subjective impressions of his will to remind and encourage us and often to prompt our thoughts in the right direction in many rapid decisions that we make throughout the day—and it is Scripture itself that tells us about these subjective factors in guidance (see Acts 16:6–7; Rom. 8:9, 14, 16; Gal. 5:16–18, 25). Yet these verses on the sufficiency of Scripture teach us that such subjective impressions can only *remind* us of moral commands that are already in Scripture, or bring to mind facts that we (in theory at least) could have known or did know otherwise; they can never add to the commands of Scripture, or replace Scripture in defining what God's will is, or equal Scripture in authority in our lives.

Because people from all kinds of Christian traditions have made serious mistakes when they felt confident that God was "leading them" to make a particular decision, it is important to remember that, except where an explicit text of Scripture applies directly to a situation, we can never have 100 percent certainty in this life that we know what God's will is in a situation. We can only have varying degrees of

requires some work, it is possible to find all the biblical passages that are directly relevant to the matters of marriage and divorce, or the responsibilities of parents to children, or the relationship between a Christian and civil government.

This doctrine means, moreover, that it is possible to collect all the passages that directly relate to doctrinal issues such as the atonement, or the person of Christ, or the work of the Holy Spirit in the believer's life today. In these and hundreds of other moral and doctrinal questions, the biblical teaching about the sufficiency of Scripture gives us confidence that we *will be able to find* what God requires us to think or to do in these areas. In many of these areas we can attain confidence that we, together with the vast majority of the church throughout history, have found and correctly formulated what God wants us to think or to do. Simply stated, the doctrine of the sufficiency of Scripture tells us that it is possible to study systematic theology and ethics and find answers to our questions.

At this point we differ from Roman Catholic theologians, who would say that we have not found all that God says to us about any particular subject until we have also listened to the official teaching of the church throughout its history. We would respond that although the history of the church may help us to *understand* what God says to us in the Bible, never in church history has God *added* to the teachings or commands of Scripture: Nowhere in church history outside of Scripture has God *added* anything that he requires us to believe or to do. Scripture is sufficient to equip us for "every good work," and to walk in its ways is to be "blameless" in God's sight.

At this point we also differ from nonevangelical theologians who are not convinced that the Bible is God's Word in any unique or absolutely authoritative sense, and who would therefore search not only the Bible but also many other early Christian writings in an attempt to find not so much *what God said* to mankind but rather *what many early Christians experienced* in their relationship with God. They would not expect to arrive at a single, unified conclusion about what God wants us to think or do with regard to any particular question, but to discover a variety of opinions and viewpoints collected around some major unifying ideas. All of the viewpoints held by early Christians in any of the early churches would then be potentially valid viewpoints for Christians to hold today as well. To this we would reply that our search for answers to theological and ethical questions is not a search to find what various believers have thought in the history of the church, but is a quest to find and understand what God himself says to us in his own words, which are found in Scripture and only in Scripture.

## C. The Amount of Scripture Given Was Sufficient at Each Stage of Redemptive History

The doctrine of the sufficiency of Scripture does not imply that *God* cannot add any more words to those he has already spoken to his people. It rather implies that *man* cannot add on his own initiative any words to those that God has already spoken. Furthermore,

confidence in different situations. Though our ability to discern God's will should increase as we grow in Christian maturity, we will inevitably make some mistakes. In this regard, I have found helpful a sentence from Edmund Clowney: "The degree of certainty we have with regard to God's will in a situation is directly proportional to the degree of clarity we have as to how the Word of God applies to the situation" (from a personal conversation, November 1992).

it implies that in fact *God has not spoken* to mankind any more words which he requires us to believe or obey other than those which we have now in the Bible.

This point is important, for it helps us to understand how God could tell his people that his words to them were sufficient at many different points in the history of redemption, and how he could nevertheless add to those words later. For example, in Deuteronomy 29:29 Moses says, "The secret things belong to the LORD our God; but the things that are revealed belong to us and to our children for ever, that we may do all the words of this law."

This verse reminds us that God has always taken the initiative in revealing things to us. He has decided what to reveal and what not to reveal. At each stage in redemptive history, the things that God had revealed were for his people for that time, and they were to study, believe, and obey those things. With further progress in the history of redemption, more of God's words were added, recording and interpreting that history (see chapter 3 above regarding the development of the canon).

Thus, at the time of the death of Moses, the first five books of our Old Testament were sufficient for God's people at that time. But God directed later authors to add more so that Scripture would be sufficient for believers in subsequent times. For Christians today, the words from God that we have in the Old and New Testaments together are sufficient for us during the church age. After the death, resurrection, and ascension of Christ, and the founding of the early church as recorded in the New Testament, and the assembling of the books of the New Testament canon, no further central redemptive acts of God in history (acts that have direct relevance for all God's people for all subsequent time) have occurred, and thus no further words of God have been given to record and interpret those acts for us.

This means that we can cite Scripture texts from throughout the canon to show that the principle of the sufficiency of God's revelation to his people at each particular time has remained the same. In this sense, these verses that talk about the sufficiency of Scripture in earlier periods are directly applicable to us as well, even though the extent of the Bible to which they refer in our situation is greater than the extent of the Scripture to which they referred in their original setting. The following texts from Scripture thus apply to us also in that sense:

> *You shall not add to the word which I command you,* nor take from it; that you may keep the commandments of the LORD your God which I command you. (Deut. 4:2)

> Everything that I command you you shall be careful to do; *you shall not add to it or take from it.* (Deut. 12:32)

> Every word of God proves true; he is a shield to those who take refuge in him. *Do not add to his words,* lest he rebuke you, and you be found a liar. (Prov. 30:5–6)

> I warn everyone who hears the words of the prophecy of this book: *if anyone adds to them,* God will add to him the plagues described in this book, and if anyone takes away from the words of the book of this prophecy, God will take

away his share in the tree of life and in the holy city, which are described in this book. (Rev. 22:18–19)[2]

## D. Practical Applications of the Sufficiency of Scripture

The doctrine of the sufficiency of Scripture has several practical applications to our Christian lives. The following list is intended to be helpful but not exhaustive.

1. The sufficiency of Scripture should encourage us as we try to discover what God would have us to *think* (about a particular doctrinal issue) or to *do* (in a particular situation). We should be encouraged that *everything* God wants to tell us about that question is to be found in Scripture. This does not mean that the Bible answers all the questions that we might think up, for "The secret things belong to the LORD our God" (Deut. 29:29). But it does mean that when we are facing a problem of genuine importance to our Christian life, we can approach Scripture with the confidence that from it God will provide us with guidance for that problem.

There will of course be some times when the answer we find is that Scripture does not speak directly to our question. (This would be the case, for example, if we tried to find from Scripture what "order of worship" to follow on Sunday mornings, or whether it is better to kneel or perhaps to stand when we pray, or at what time we should eat our meals during the day, etc.) In those cases, we may conclude that God has not required us to think or to act in any certain way with regard to that question (except, perhaps, in terms of more general principles regarding our attitudes and goals). But in many other cases we will find direct and clear guidance from the Lord to equip us for "every good work" (2 Tim. 3:17).

As we go through life, frequent practice in searching Scripture for guidance will result in an increasing ability to find accurate, carefully formulated answers to our problems and questions. Lifelong growth in understanding Scripture will thus include growth in the skill of rightly understanding the Bible's teachings and applying them to specific questions.

2. The sufficiency of Scripture reminds us that *we are to add nothing to Scripture,* and that *we are to consider no other writings of equal value to Scripture.* This principle is violated by almost all cults and sects. Mormons, for example, claim to believe the Bible, but they also claim divine authority for the *Book of Mormon.* Christian Scientists similarly claim to believe the Bible, but in practice they hold the book *Science and Health With a Key to the Scriptures,* by Mary Baker Eddy, on a par with Scripture or above it in authority. Since these claims violate God's commands not to add to his words, we should not think that any additional words from God to us would be found in these writings. Even in Christian churches a similar error is sometimes made when people go beyond what Scripture says and assert with great confidence new ideas about God or heaven, basing their teachings not on Scripture but on their own speculation or even on claimed experiences of dying and coming back to life.

---

[2]The primary reference of this verse is of course to the book of Revelation itself, but its placement here at the very end of the only book that could come last in the New Testament canon can hardly be accidental. Thus, a secondary application of this verse to the entire canon does not seem inappropriate (see the discussion in chapter 3, pp. 50–51).

3. The sufficiency of Scripture also tells us that *God does not require us to believe anything about himself or his redemptive work that is not found in Scripture.* Among writings from the time of the early church are some collections of alleged sayings of Jesus that were not preserved in the Gospels. It is likely that at least some of the "sayings of Jesus" found in these writings are rather accurate records of things Jesus actually said (though it is now impossible for us to determine with any high degree of probability which sayings those are). But it does not really matter at all for our Christian lives if we never read any of those sayings, for God has caused to be recorded in Scripture everything that we need to know about Jesus' words and deeds in order to trust and obey him perfectly. Though these collections of sayings do have some limited value in linguistic research and perhaps in the study of the history of the church, they are of no direct value whatever for us in learning what we should believe about the life and teachings of Christ, or in formulating our doctrinal or ethical convictions.

4. The sufficiency of Scripture shows us that *no modern revelations from God are to be placed on a level equal to Scripture in authority.* At various times throughout the history of the church, and particularly in the modern charismatic movement, people have claimed that God has given revelations through them for the benefit of the church. However we may evaluate such claims, we must be careful never to allow (in theory or in practice) the placing of such revelations on a level equal to Scripture.[3] We must insist that God does not require us to believe anything about himself or his work in the world that is contained in these revelations but not in Scripture. And we must insist that God does not require us to obey any moral directives that come to us through such means but that are not confirmed by Scripture. The Bible contains all the words of God we need for trusting and obeying him perfectly.[4]

It should also be noted at this point that whenever challenges to the sufficiency of Scripture have come in the form of other documents to be placed alongside Scripture (whether from extrabiblical Christian literature of the first century or from the accumulated teachings of the Roman Catholic Church, or from the books of various cults such as the *Book of Mormon*), the result has always been (1) to deemphasize the teachings of the Bible itself and (2) to begin to teach some things that are contrary to Scripture. This is a danger of which the church must constantly be aware.

5. With regard to living the Christian life, the sufficiency of Scripture reminds us that *nothing is sin that is not forbidden by Scripture either explicitly or by implication.* To walk in the law of the Lord is to be "blameless" (Ps. 119:1). Therefore we are not to add prohibitions to those already stated in Scripture. From time to time there may be situations in which it would be wrong, for example, for an individual Christian to drink coffee or Coca-Cola, or to attend movie theaters, or to eat meat offered to idols (see 1 Cor. 8–10), but unless some

---

[3]In fact, the more responsible spokesmen for the modern charismatic movement seem generally to agree with this caution: see Wayne Grudem, *The Gift of Prophecy in the New Testament and Today* (Eastbourne, England: Kingsway, and Westchester, Ill.: Crossway, 1988), pp. 110–12; 245–50.

[4]I do not wish to imply at this point that I am adopting a "cessationist" view of spiritual gifts (that is, a view that holds that certain gifts, such as prophecy and speaking in tongues, ceased when the apostles died). I only wish at this point to state that there is a danger in explicitly or even implicitly giving these gifts a status that effectively challenges the authority or the sufficiency of Scripture in Christians' lives. More detailed discussion of these gifts is given in Grudem, *The Gift of Prophecy in the New Testament and Today* (see n. 3 above).

specific teaching or some general principle of Scripture can be shown to prohibit these (or any other activities) for all believers for all time, we must insist that these activities are not in themselves sinful and they are not in all situations prohibited by God for his people.[5]

This also is an important principle because there is always the tendency among believers to begin to neglect the regular daily searching of Scripture for guidance and to begin to live by a set of written or unwritten rules (or denominational traditions) concerning what one does or does not do in the Christian life.

Furthermore, whenever we add to the list of sins that are prohibited by Scripture itself, there will be harm to the church and to the lives of individual believers. The Holy Spirit will not empower obedience to rules that do not have God's approval from Scripture, nor will believers generally find delight in obedience to commands that do not accord with the laws of God written on their hearts. In some cases, Christians may repeatedly and earnestly plead with God for "victory" over supposed sins that are in fact no sins at all, yet no "victory" will be given, for the attitude or action in question is in fact not a sin and is not displeasing to God. Great discouragement in prayer and frustration in the Christian life generally may be the outcome.

In other cases, continued or even increasing disobedience to these new "sins" will result, together with a false sense of guilt and a resulting alienation from God. Often there arises an increasingly uncompromising and legalistic insistence on these new rules on the part of those who *do* follow them, and genuine fellowship among believers in the church will fade away. Evangelism will often be stifled, for the silent proclamation of the gospel that comes from the lives of believers will at least *seem* (to outsiders) to include the additional requirement that one must fit this uniform pattern of life in order to become a member of the body of Christ.

One clear example of such an addition to the commands of Scripture is found in the opposition of the Roman Catholic Church to "artificial" methods of birth control, a policy that finds no valid support in Scripture. Widespread disobedience, alienation, and false guilt have been the result. Yet such is the propensity of human nature to make such rules that other examples can probably be found in the written or unwritten traditions of almost every denomination.

6. The sufficiency of Scripture also tells us that *nothing is required of us by God that is not commanded in Scripture either explicitly or by implication.* This reminds us that the focus of our search for God's will ought to be on Scripture, rather than on seeking guidance through prayer for changed circumstances or altered feelings or direct guidance from the Holy Spirit

---

[5]Of course, human societies such as nations, churches, families, etc. can make rules for the conduct of their own affairs (such as "Children in this family may not watch television on weeknights"). No such rule can be found in Scripture, nor is it likely that such a rule could be demonstrated by implication from the principles of Scripture. Yet obedience to these rules is required by God because Scripture tells us to be subject to governing authorities (Rom. 13:1–7; 1 Peter 2:13–3:6, et al.). A denial of the sufficiency of Scripture would occur only if someone attempted to give the rule a generalized application outside of the situation in which it should appropriately function ("No member of our church should watch TV on weeknights" or "No Christian should watch TV on weeknights"). In such a case it has become not a rule for conduct in one specific situation but a moral command apparently intended to apply to all Christians no matter what their situation. We are not free to add such rules to Scripture and to attempt to impose them on all the believers over whom we have influence, nor can the church as a whole attempt to do this. (Here again, Roman Catholics would differ and would say that God gives to the church the authority to impose moral rules in addition to Scripture on all the members of the church.)

apart from Scripture. It also means that if someone *claims* to have a message from God telling us what we ought to do, we need never assume that it is sin to disobey such a message unless it can be confirmed by the application of Scripture itself to our situation.

The discovery of this great truth could bring tremendous joy and peace to the lives of thousands of Christians who, spending countless hours seeking God's will outside of Scripture, are often uncertain about whether they have found it. In fact, many Christians today have very little confidence in their ability to discover God's will with any degree of certainty. Thus, there is little striving to do God's will (for who can know it?) and little growth in holiness before God.

The opposite ought to be true. Christians who are convinced of the sufficiency of Scripture should begin eagerly to seek and find God's will in Scripture. They should be eagerly and regularly growing in obedience to God, knowing great freedom and peace in the Christian life. Then they would be able to say with the psalmist:

> I will keep your law continually,
> for ever and ever;
> and *I shall walk at liberty,*
> *for I have sought your precepts. . . .*
>
> *Great peace have those who love your law;*
> nothing can make them stumble. (Ps. 119:44–45, 165)

7. The sufficiency of Scripture reminds us that in our doctrinal and ethical teaching we should *emphasize what Scripture emphasizes and be content with what God has told us in Scripture.* There are some subjects about which God has told us little or nothing in the Bible. We must remember that "The secret things belong to the LORD our God" (Deut. 29:29) and that God has revealed to us in Scripture exactly what he deemed right for us. We must accept this and not think that Scripture is something less than it should be, or begin to wish that God had given us much more information about subjects on which there are very few scriptural references. Of course, there will be some situations where we are confronted with a particular problem that requires a great deal of attention, far greater than the emphasis that it receives in the teaching of Scripture. But those situations should be relatively infrequent and should not be representative of the general course of our lives or ministries.

It is characteristic of many cults that they emphasize obscure portions or teachings of Scripture (one thinks of the Mormon emphasis on baptism for the dead, a subject that is mentioned in only one verse in the Bible [1 Cor. 15:29], in a phrase whose exact meaning is apparently impossible now to determine with certainty). But a similar error was made by an entire generation of liberal New Testament scholars in the earlier part of this century, who devoted most of their scholarly lives to a futile search for the sources "behind" our present gospel narratives or to a search for the "authentic" sayings of Jesus.

Unfortunately, a similar pattern has too often occurred among evangelicals within various denominations. The doctrinal matters that have divided evangelical Protestant denominations from one another have almost uniformly been matters on which the Bible places relatively little emphasis, and matters in which our conclusions must be drawn from skillful inference much more than from direct biblical statements. For example, abiding denominational differences have occurred or have been maintained over the "proper" form of church government, the exact nature of Christ's presence in the Lord's Supper, the exact sequence of the events surrounding Christ's return, the categories of persons who should be admitted to the Lord's Supper, the way in which God planned that the merits of Christ's death would be applied to believers and not applied to unbelievers, the proper subjects for baptism, the correct understanding of the "baptism in the Holy Spirit," and so forth.

We should not say that these issues are all unimportant, nor should we say that Scripture gives no solution to any of them. However, since all of these topics receive *relatively little direct emphasis in Scripture,* it is ironic and tragic that denominational leaders will so often give much of their lives to defending precisely the minor doctrinal points that make their denominations different from others. Is such effort really motivated by a desire to bring unity of understanding to the church, or might it stem in some measure from human pride, a desire to retain power over others, and an attempt at self-justification, which is displeasing to God and ultimately unedifying to the church?

## QUESTIONS FOR PERSONAL APPLICATION

1. In the process of growing in the Christian life and deepening your relationship with God, approximately how much emphasis have you placed on reading the Bible itself and how much on reading other Christian books? In seeking to know God's will for your daily life, what is the relative emphasis you have put on reading Scripture itself and on reading other Christian books? Do you think the doctrine of the sufficiency of Scripture will cause you to place more emphasis on reading Scripture itself?

2. What are some of the doctrinal or moral questions you are wondering about? Has this chapter increased your confidence in the ability of Scripture to provide a clear answer for some of those questions?

3. Have you ever wished that the Bible would say more than it does about a certain subject? Or less? What do you think motivated that wish? After reading this chapter, how would you approach someone who expressed such a wish today? How is God's wisdom shown in the fact that he chose not to make the Bible a great deal longer or a great deal shorter than it actually is?

4. If the Bible contains everything we need God to tell us for obeying him perfectly, what is the role of the following in helping us to find God's will for ourselves: advice from others; sermons or Bible classes; our consciences; our feelings; the leading of the Holy Spirit as we sense him prompting our inward desires and subjective impressions; changes in circumstances; the gift of prophecy (if you think it can function today)?

5. In the light of this chapter, how would you find God's "perfect" will for your life? Is it possible that there would be more than one "perfect" choice in many decisions we make? (Consider Ps. 1:3 and 1 Cor. 7:39 in seeking an answer.)

6. Have there been times when you have understood the principles of Scripture well enough with regard to a specific situation but have not known the facts of the situation well enough to know how to apply those scriptural principles correctly? In seeking to know God's will, can there be any other things we need to know except (a) the teaching of Scripture and (b) the facts of the situation in question, together with (c) skill in applying (a) to (b) correctly? What then is the role of prayer in seeking guidance? What should we pray for?

## SPECIAL TERMS

blameless
sufficiency of Scripture

## BIBLIOGRAPHY

Friesen, Garry, and J. Robin Maxson. *Decision Making and the Will of God.* Portland, Ore.: Multnomah, 1981.
Packer, J. I. "Scripture." In *NDT,* pp. 627–31.
Weeks, Noel. *The Sufficiency of Scripture.* Edinburgh and Carlisle, Pa.: Banner of Truth, 1988.

## SCRIPTURE MEMORY PASSAGE

**Psalm 119:1:** *Blessed are those whose way is blameless, who walk in the law of the Lord!*

## HYMN

### "How Firm a Foundation"

Few if any hymns deal specifically with the sufficiency of Scripture, perhaps because Christians have failed to realize the great comfort and peace that this doctrine brings to the Christian life. But the first verse of the following hymn contains a statement of this doctrine. It begins by telling us that God has laid a firm foundation for our faith in his Word. Then it says, "What more can he say than to you he hath said . . . ?" The rich and full promises of God throughout Scripture are sufficient for our every need in every circumstance. This should be great cause for rejoicing! The subsequent verses contain quotations, paraphrases, and allusions to promises of God that are scattered throughout Scripture, many of them from Isaiah. Verses 2–6 are all written as sentences that are spoken by God to us, and when we sing them we should think of ourselves singing the words of God's promises to others in the congregation for their comfort and encouragement.

How firm a foundation, ye saints of the Lord,
Is laid for your faith in his excellent Word!

What more can he say than to you he hath said,
    You who unto Jesus for refuge have fled?
    You who unto Jesus for refuge have fled?

"Fear not, I am with thee, O be not dismayed;
    I, I am thy God, and will still give thee aid;
I'll strengthen thee, help thee, and cause thee to stand,
    Upheld by my righteous, omnipotent hand,
    Upheld by my righteous, omnipotent hand.

"When through the deep waters I call thee to go,
    The rivers of woe shall not thee overflow;
For I will be with thee thy troubles to bless,
    And sanctify to thee thy deepest distress,
    And sanctify to thee thy deepest distress.

"When through fiery trials thy pathway shall lie,
    My grace, all sufficient, shall be thy supply;
The flame shall not hurt thee; I only design
    Thy dross to consume, and thy gold to refine,
    Thy dross to consume, and thy gold to refine.

"E'en down to old age all my people shall prove
    My sovereign, eternal, unchangeable love;
And when hoary hairs shall their temples adorn,
    Like lambs they shall still in my bosom be borne,
    Like lambs they shall still in my bosom be borne.

"The soul that on Jesus hath leaned for repose,
    I will not, I will not desert to his foes;
That soul, though all hell should endeavor to shake,
    I'll never, no, never, no, never forsake,
    I'll never, no, never, no, never forsake."

FROM: RIPPON'S *SELECTION OF HYMNS*, 1787